CANNING MASTERY

A COMPREHENSIVE GUIDE FOR BEGINNERS IN VARIOUS TECHNIQUES OF FOOD PRESERVATION

CALEB QUINN

TABLE OF CONTENTS

INTRODUCTION

Thinking back to my younger days, I remember the sweet aroma of homemade strawberry jam wafting through my grandmother's kitchen on a lazy summer morning. That comforting fragrance, so redolent of love, family, and tradition, used to envelop me as a child during those cherished visits to her home.

It wasn't just about the jam but everything it represented: the hours spent together in the sunlit strawberry fields, the stories shared over breakfast toast slathered with that very jam, and the unbreakable bond that formed between us, anchored by this shared experience.

In today's fast-paced world, we find ourselves increasingly disconnected from the sources of our food, yearning for a return to the simplicity and authenticity of days gone by. You, like many, may feel a sense of vulnerability and loss of control in an overly commercialized food system. Concerns about food quality, safety, and sustainability are all too real.

The desire to embark on the journey of canning and food preservation is strong, yet the wealth of information available can be overwhelming.

How do you discern reliable sources from outdated or incorrect advice?

How do you ensure that your canned goods are safe for consumption, avoiding the specter of botulism and spoilage?

The initial cost of specific canning equipment can be a barrier for some, especially if you're on a tight budget.

And then there's the issue of time, a precious commodity in our busy lives. Can you find the hours required for proper canning, especially when dealing with larger batches or more complex recipes?

You see, I understand your concerns and your yearning for a more hands-on, sustainable approach to the food on your table. I know how intimidating it can be to step into the world of canning, with its risks and complexities, and I'm here to help you take that first step.

You'll discover the shortcuts you need to navigate the world of canning and food preservation. Let me introduce the first shortcut, the CAN-DO Model: Canning, Acidity, Nutrition, Durability, and Organization. This model is designed to simplify your journey and ensure your canned goods are not only safe but also nutritious and delicious.

- **Canning**: This is the core of the process. It involves properly sealing and preserving food in jars to extend its shelf life. Understanding the canning process is essential—whether it's water bath canning for high-acid foods or pressure canning for low-acid foods. This step ensures the long-term preservation and safety of your food.
- **Acidity:** Acidity plays a pivotal role in canning. High-acid foods, like fruits, most tomatoes, and some pickled products, can be safely processed using the water bath canning method. Low-acid foods, such as vegetables and meats, require pressure canning to ensure they reach the necessary temperatures for safe preservation. Recognizing the acidity of the foods you're preserving is crucial to selecting the appropriate canning method.
- **Nutrition**: Preserving the nutritional value of your canned goods is a vital aspect of home canning. While some nutrient loss is inevitable during the canning process, understanding how to minimize it is essential. Proper preparation, selecting the best quality produce, and following canning procedures carefully can help retain as many nutrients as possible.
- **Durability**: This element emphasizes ensuring the longevity of your canned goods. Proper sealing, choosing the right jars and lids, and storing canned items in optimal conditions help maintain their quality and safety over time. Additionally, labeling and organizing your canned goods can further enhance their durability, allowing you to use older items first through a first-in, first-out (FIFO) approach.

- **Organization**: Effective organization is the cornerstone of a successful home canning process. It starts with gathering the necessary tools and equipment and having a well-organized canning space. Properly labeling your canned goods with information such as the food product and the date of canning ensures you can easily identify and use your preserves. This organization streamlines the canning process for safety and efficiency.

The CAN-DO Model serves as a guide to help you navigate the world of canning and food preservation. By incorporating these five principles into your canning practices, you can feel confident that your canned goods will not only be safe but also delicious and nutritious. It simplifies your journey and empowers you to create a well-organized, efficient, and sustainable approach to preserving the flavors of the seasons all year round.

Still not convinced? Take a look at the extreme testimonials of those who have transformed their lives using this model:

- "Before I discovered the CAN-DO Model, my family's diet was full of unhealthy, store-bought processed foods. But after embracing canning and following the model, we've transitioned to a diet rich in home-preserved fruits and vegetables. The nutrition element of the model made all the difference, and my family's health has transformed. We've seen remarkable improvements in our well-being, and our doctor couldn't be happier."

- "I used to struggle with my grocery bills, constantly worried about the rising cost of fresh produce. Then, I learned about the CAN-DO Model, which emphasizes durability. I started canning, and my pantry now overflows with home-preserved goods. Not only do I save a ton on groceries, but I've also started selling my canned creations at local markets. It's not just a hobby anymore; it's a side business that's boosted my income significantly."

- "My family was growing apart in our fast-paced lives. We rarely sat down for meals together, and the connection we once had was fading. Thanks to the organization aspect of the CAN-DO Model, we've not only started canning together but also started preserving our cherished family recipes. It's become a tradition that brings us together regularly. Our bond is stronger than ever, and we're creating new memories with every batch we can."

- "Sustainability and reducing our carbon footprint were always close to my heart, but I struggled to find a way to make a real impact. Then, I started using the CAN-DO Model. By canning and preserving local, seasonal produce, I've cut down on food waste, supported local farmers, and reduced the need for industrial food production. I feel like a true eco-warrior, making a difference every day."

- "Cooking was never my forte, and I often relied on pre-packaged meals. However, the CAN-DO Model has transformed me into a confident home chef. With a pantry full of my canned goods, I can create gourmet dishes using my preserved ingredients. I've even won a few cooking competitions, something I'd never imagined before. Canning has turned me into a master chef."

These testimonials showcase how the CAN-DO Model can impact various aspects of people's lives, from health and finances to family bonds and personal growth. They reflect the potential for profound change through the practice of home canning and food preservation following the CAN-DO Model.

Imagine the result: your pantry shelves lined with vibrant, home-preserved goods, the taste of everyone's grandmother's strawberry jam on your breakfast table every day, and the peace of mind that comes from knowing you've reclaimed control over your food.

As your guide, I've spent years perfecting the art of canning, learning from the ground up, making mistakes, and fine-tuning the process until it's foolproof. I'm here to share the secrets and techniques that have made a world of difference in my own life.

Before discovering this new information, I too struggled with the complexities of canning, wasted time and resources, and felt that loss of control in the food system. But I've come through to the other side, and I'm here to help you do the same.

You are in the right place. This is not just a book; it's a key to a better, more connected, and more empowered life. So, let's embark on this journey together, and soon, you'll be savoring the taste of homemade preserves that carry the essence of your memories and the promise of a brighter, more self-reliant future.

1

A TIMELESS TRADITION

Have you ever stopped and thought about how people way back when stored and preserved their food? I mean, how in the world did they make their food last before refrigerators? It's actually a very captivating thought and an interesting journey.

When we start to think about it, without a way to preserve our food, we wouldn't have jams, jellies, canned goods, and all the other items we have come to enjoy on a daily basis.

Food preservation plays a very big part in our lives, but where did it all start? Well, let's look into some preservation history, find out why canning is on the comeback in the modern world, and discover all the benefits it holds (and yes, it is much more than just being able to enjoy your favorite fruits and veggies all year long). Let's also bust some common canning myths.

CAN-DO MODEL: CANNING—THE TIMELESS ART OF PRESERVATION

Food preservation is a practice as old as humanity itself. Our ancestors, facing the challenge of food spoilage, developed ingenious methods to ensure sustenance during lean times and to savor the bounty of their harvests. The history of food preservation is a tapestry woven with creativity, resourcefulness, and necessity.

Sun Drying

First stop, around 4,000 B.C.E., when our early foodie friends discovered sun drying. This OG method involved simply plopping food out in the sun, letting the heat do its thing to zap that moisture. It sounds great, right? But it had its quirks, like being completely at the mercy of the weather and needing an eagle eye to avoid any mishaps.

Jams and Jellies

Fast forward a bit, and we're in the land of jams and jellies. Folks back in the day figured out that dunking food in honey was like a sweet ticket to preservation town. We're talking recipes dating back to the first century!

Curing

Around 1400, enter the classic cure. No, not the cure for the common cold, but food preservation by dunking it in a salty bath, aka brine. Picture food swimming around in there while the magic happens through something called osmosis. Water's drawn out of the food, and voilà! It's preserved, and it still tastes awesome.

Freezing

So, you might think refrigeration is a modern marvel. Well, it was an ancient secret, too! It goes way back to when communities stashed their food under ice or in icehouses during frosty times—but we'll get to the modern fridge in a bit.

Canning

Now, let's jump to the late 18th century, when canning as we know it first hit the scene. French scientist Nicolas Appert was the headliner here, sealing food in containers, giving it a steamy treatment, and creating an airtight fortress against pesky microorganisms.

Pasteurization

Louis Pasteur, the legend himself, unveiled pasteurization in 1862. This method involves sealing food in containers and heating it to give those tiny troublemakers—microorganisms— a run for their money.

Dehydration

Fast-forward to the 1940s, and we're embracing dehydration. This is like the upgraded version of sun drying, thanks to electrical food dehydrators. You're left with lightweight, mineral-rich foods that can jazz up your meals.

Vacuum Packaging

Come the mid-1950s, German whiz Karl Busch introduced vacuum packaging. Picture your food snuggling up in airtight bags, with vacuum sealers kicking oxygen out of the party, making sure bacteria don't crash it.

Irradiation

About that 1905 discovery? It's called food irradiation, and it's all about using radiation to send bacteria packing. This technique became super popular in the mid-20th century, especially for safeguarding meats and spices.

Chemical Preservatives

Last but not least, think ancient times when our kitchen heroes used vinegar and other bits and bobs to fend off food nasties. These preservatives weren't about changing taste but more like bodyguards against bacterial invaders. Think of it as vinegar's gig in the pickling world.

As we've seen, humans have always been innovative when it comes to preserving food. From salting meats to fermenting vegetables, our ancestors had their tricks. This book is all about bringing canning and food preservation to modern times. We'll not only explore the historical significance of these techniques but also equip you with the knowledge and skills to continue this time-honored tradition in your kitchen. So, let's embark on this culinary journey through time and discover the art of canning—a timeless method that connects us with our heritage and empowers us to take control of our food's quality, safety, and sustainability.

CANNING IN THE MODERN KITCHEN: A TASTE OF THE GOOD OLD DAYS

Canning is a fantastic culinary craft that deserves a place of honor in your kitchen. It's all about preserving food by packing it into airtight containers and giving it a little heat treatment. The magic happens when you create a tight seal that keeps out the air and any pesky microorganisms. The result? Your food stays fresh, flavorful, and safe for much longer, even without refrigeration. Let's dive deeper into why canning is having its modern-day moment.

1. Smart savings

Money matters, and canning is a money-saver's dream. When you have an abundance of seasonal fruits and veggies, why not buy them in bulk and can your own goodies? It's a budget-friendly move, and homemade canned food is often way cheaper than store-bought stuff.

2. Quality control

In a world where we're all about knowing what goes into our bodies, canning lets you take charge. You pick the ingredients, and that means pure, unadulterated, and wholesome food. No mystery additives, just straightforward, honest flavors.

3. Eco-friendly living

The environment is close to our hearts, and canning is a way to show it some love. By using local, seasonal produce, you're reducing the carbon footprint associated with transporting and packaging food. It's a green choice that helps support local agriculture and cuts down on unnecessary packaging.

4. Food safety

Food scares and recalls can be downright scary. Canning is your safety net. When done correctly, it's like a fortress against spoilage and contamination. Your canned treasures stay safe to enjoy whenever you like.

5. DIY fun

Are you a fan of hands-on projects? Canning is your opportunity to get crafty in the kitchen. It puts you in control of your food supply and cuts your reliance on mass-produced products.

That sense of accomplishment and self-reliance is both empowering and fun.

Canning isn't only about preserving food; it's also about preserving a way of life. It's a tribute to our ancestors, who used these methods to ensure they had enough to eat throughout the year. When you're canning, you're part of a culinary heritage that goes back generations.

Our lives are busier than ever, and canning bridges the gap between time-honored traditions and the need for convenience. Thanks to modern canning equipment and techniques, the process is more accessible and quicker than you might think.

Canning isn't only about preserving traditions; it's also about making smart choices for your health and the planet. It's an opportunity to create healthier meals using local, environmentally friendly ingredients while keeping up with the demands of modern living. In a nutshell, you get all the benefits of tradition and the convenience of modernity. It's not just about food—it's a journey through time and an adventure in sustainability, self-sufficiency, and culinary heritage.

The resurgence of canning in the modern kitchen is a delicious way to harmonize tradition and modernity in your culinary journey. Ready to give it a try? Before you grab those jars, flex those cooking muscles, and dive into the wonderful world of canning, let's first look at all the wonderful perks there are.

THE MANY PERKS OF CANNING

Canning your own food isn't just a practical endeavor; it's a multifaceted journey filled with numerous benefits that enrich your life in more ways than one. Let's explore 12 advantages, each with a compelling reason to embrace the art of canning.

1. Eating real food

In a world inundated with processed and artificial foods, canning allows you to reconnect with real food. You'll savor the authentic flavors of seasonal produce and enjoy the simple pleasure of homemade goods.

2. Controlling the ingredients

When you can your own food, you have complete control over what goes into your jars. You can choose to ditch excessive salt and sugar, ensuring that your preserves align with your dietary preferences and health goals.

3. Improving your diet

Canning empowers you to make healthier choices. You can prioritize organic, locally sourced, and fresh ingredients, resulting in a diet that's not only delicious but also nutritious.

4. Protecting the planet

By canning your own food, you reduce your reliance on commercial products with excessive packaging. This eco-friendly practice helps lower your carbon dioxide footprint, contributing to a more sustainable future.

5. Saving some cash

Canning is a cost-effective way to stock your pantry with quality staples. You'll reduce food waste, save money in the long run, and enjoy the economic benefits of preserving your own food.

6. Supporting the local economy

When you source your produce from local farmers and markets for canning, you contribute to the growth of your community's economy, ensuring that your food dollars stay close to home.

7. Making dinner a snap

Having canned goods on hand makes meal preparation a breeze. Whether it's for a quick weeknight dinner or an impromptu gathering, your homemade treasures will come to the rescue.

8. Enjoying a meaningful hobby

Canning isn't a chore; it's a fulfilling hobby. The process of preserving food can be both meditative and creative, offering a sense of accomplishment and satisfaction.

9. Becoming self-sufficient

In an age where self-sufficiency is often overlooked, canning rekindles the spirit of independence. You'll feel more secure in your ability to provide for your family.

10. Tapping your creative side

Canning allows you to explore your culinary creativity. You can experiment with flavors, combinations, and techniques, resulting in unique, personalized preserves.

11. Sharing your handmade treasures

There's immense joy in sharing the fruits of your labor with friends and family. Canned goods make thoughtful, heartfelt gifts that showcase your dedication and care.

12. Anticipating a fruitful journey

The canning process is a journey filled with anticipation. From the planting and harvesting to the preservation and enjoyment, it's a cycle that connects you with the seasons and the natural world.

Each of these perks makes canning not just a practical skill but a rewarding and enriching part of your life. By embracing the art of canning, you unlock a world of possibilities, from healthier eating to contributing to a more sustainable future. So, get ready to embark on a journey that not only fills your pantry but also enriches your soul.

BUSTING CANNING MYTHS

Canning is an art that's been practiced for generations, passed down through families, and cherished for its ability to preserve the flavors of the season. However, along the way, several myths and misconceptions have taken root, leading many to make potentially dangerous mistakes. Let's address and debunk these common canning myths, ensuring that you have the knowledge and confidence to safely and successfully preserve your own food.

Myth 1: If It's Canned in the Store, You Can "Can" It at Home

This myth couldn't be further from the truth, as commercial canning processes are vastly different from home canning methods. Store-bought canned goods undergo rigorous quality control and safety checks that are hard to replicate in a home kitchen. Not all foods are suitable for home canning, and safe practices must be followed.

- Commercial canning processes are highly regulated, involving industrial-grade equipment and quality control measures.

- Store-bought canned goods often undergo additional safety checks, including microbiological testing.
- Home canning requires specific methods and recipes designed for safe preservation.
- Not all foods can be safely canned at home, especially low-acid foods like vegetables and meats.

Myth 2: My Grandmother and Great-Grandmother Canned This Way for Years, and They Never Got Sick

While your grandmother and great-grandmother may have indeed practiced canning for years, the understanding of food safety has evolved. Modern research and insights have highlighted the risks associated with certain practices that were once considered safe. To ensure your safety and that of your loved ones, it's important to adopt up-to-date canning methods.

- While your ancestors may have canned, the understanding of food safety has evolved.
- Modern research has identified potential health risks associated with outdated canning practices.
- Following up-to-date canning guidelines ensures food safety and protects against foodborne illnesses.

Myth 3: Oven Canning Is Just Fine; It's the Same Temperature as Boiling Water, After All

Oven canning is a highly debated practice that many experts advise against. While it might seem similar to boiling water canning, the temperature control and distribution in an oven can be inconsistent and unreliable. This can result in improperly canned food, putting your health at risk.

- Oven canning can lead to uneven heating and temperature fluctuations, which may result in underprocessing or overprocessing.
- Boiling water canning has precise temperature control, ensuring the destruction of harmful microorganisms.
- Oven canning is generally not recommended due to safety concerns.

Myth 4: My Jar Sealed, So I'm Good to Go

While a sealed jar is a positive sign, it doesn't guarantee the safety of the contents. Proper canning requires not only a sealed jar but also a correct processing method and thorough sterilization to kill harmful microorganisms.

- While a sealed jar is a positive sign, it's only one part of the canning process.
- Proper canning involves heating food to the correct temperature to kill microorganisms and create a vacuum seal.
- A sealed jar may not guarantee that the food inside is processed correctly and safely.

Myth 5: Just Scrape the Mold From the Jam/Jelly and Eat the Rest

Mold is not always confined to the visible surface. Consuming moldy food can be risky, as mold can produce toxins that spread throughout the product, even if you can't see it. Moldy jam or jelly should be discarded, not salvaged.

- Mold can produce mycotoxins, which can spread throughout the product, making it unsafe to consume.
- Moldy food should be discarded to avoid the risk of mycotoxin ingestion.
- Proper canning techniques, including sterilization, minimize the risk of mold growth.

Myth 6: Canning Is Dangerous

Canning is not inherently dangerous if you follow safe practices. With the right knowledge and precautions, canning can be a safe and rewarding experience.

- Canning, when done following recommended practices, is a safe method for food preservation.
- Canning safety involves using proper canning equipment, sterilizing jars, following tested recipes, and processing food at the correct temperatures.
- Safe canning practices have been developed and refined over time to ensure food safety.

Myth 7: You Have to Grow a Lot of Food to Make Canning Worthwhile

Canning is adaptable to your needs, whether you have a small garden or access to a bountiful harvest. You can preserve as little or as much as you like, making it a flexible and cost-effective way to manage your food supply.

- Canning is adaptable and can be scaled to your needs, whether you have a small garden or access to local produce.
- Small batches of canned goods can be a practical and cost-effective way to preserve seasonal ingredients.
- Canning allows you to reduce food waste and save money by extending the shelf life of your favorite foods.

Myth 8: You Can Get Sick or Die of Botulism from Water Bath Canning

While water bath canning is considered safe for certain foods, it is not suitable for low-acid items, which can pose a risk of botulism. We'll delve into the critical importance of acidity in the next chapter.

- Water bath canning is a safe method for preserving high-acid foods, such as fruits and tomatoes.
- Low-acid foods, like vegetables and meats, require pressure canning to eliminate the risk of botulism.
- The acidity of the food determines the appropriate canning method for safety.

By understanding these myths and the reasons behind them, you'll be better equipped to navigate the world of canning safely and confidently.

Now that we've dispelled these myths, you can proceed with confidence, knowing that you'll be following the safest and most effective canning practices. In the next chapter, "The Acid Factor," we'll explore the crucial role of acidity in canning, a fundamental aspect of ensuring your canned goods remain safe for consumption.

2

THE ACID FACTOR

D o you know a quick way to determine if a food is acidic or not? In general, the taste can be a telling indicator. Acidic foods typically have a sour taste, while alkaline ones lean toward bitterness. But what exactly is the science behind this sourness, and how does it relate to safe and effective canning? That's what we're going to delve into in this chapter.

CAN-DO MODEL: ACIDITY—THE SCIENCE BEHIND SAFE CANNING

To truly understand canning and its principles, we must first explore the foundational concepts of acidity and pH. Acidity is a fundamental characteristic of foods, and pH, short for "potential of hydrogen," is the measure of acidity or alkalinity. In canning, these factors are of utmost importance.

Acidity is a fundamental property of foods and beverages. It is characterized by the presence of acids, which are compounds that can donate protons (hydrogen ions) to a solution. This property is key to understanding how canning works.

The pH scale is a measure of the acidity or alkalinity of a substance and ranges from 0 to 14. A pH of 7 is considered neutral, while values below 7 indicate acidity and values above 7 indicate alkalinity. In canning, we are particularly concerned with foods falling on the acidic side of the pH scale.

The science behind canning is rooted in the impact of acidity on food preservation. When you have an acidic environment, with a pH level below 4.6, it creates a hostile territory for harmful microorganisms. These microorganisms, which include bacteria, yeasts, and molds, are unable to thrive or reproduce in this acidic setting. This is why foods with a pH level below 4.6 are deemed suitable for water bath canning. It's worth noting that high-acid foods, such as fruits, fruit juices, and pickled products, typically fall into this category.

Clostridium botulinum is a bacterium that can produce a deadly toxin responsible for botulism. It's a significant concern in canning. When the pH level of a food product is low (acidic), this bacterium cannot grow or produce its dangerous toxin. Therefore, maintaining proper acidity levels is critical in preventing the growth of Clostridium botulinum in canned goods. It's essential to know which foods require high acidity to remain safe and follow recommended canning methods to ensure they are below the 4.6 pH threshold.

Aside from preserving foods by creating an inhospitable environment for microorganisms, acidity also plays a pivotal role in maintaining the quality of preserved foods. It helps inactivate enzymes that naturally occur in fruits and vegetables, which can lead to spoilage or undesirable changes in color, flavor, and texture. This enzyme inactivation ensures that your canned goods not only remain safe from contamination but also retain their quality and appeal over time.

Understanding the relationship between acidity and food safety is paramount in canning. Incorrect acidity levels can lead to unsafe or spoiled products. When canning, it's crucial to distinguish between high-acid and low-acid foods and apply the appropriate canning methods and acid adjustments accordingly. The dangers of failing to address acidity issues should not be underestimated, making it essential to adhere to recommended canning practices to protect your health and the quality of your preserved foods. The CAN-DO Model, with its emphasis on acidity and pH, is a foundational concept that ensures your canning endeavors are safe and successful.

High vs. Low: Understanding the Distinction in Canning

High-acid foods are those with a natural pH level of 4.6 or lower and are characterized by their tangy or tart taste, which is due to their high acid content. Examples of high-acid foods include most fruits, tomatoes, and foods that contain added vinegar or lemon juice. The high acidity of these foods creates an environment that is hostile to the growth of harmful microorganisms, particularly Clostridium botulinum, the bacterium responsible for botulism.

When canning high-acid foods, such as jams or pickles, you're in luck because they can be safely preserved using the water bath canning method. Water bath canning effectively pasteurizes these foods, making them safe for long-term storage. The process usually involves boiling the filled jars for a specific duration, depending on the type of food, ensuring that it's heated sufficiently to destroy any potential spoilers. The acid in these foods, along with the heat, acts as a double barrier to microbial growth.

Canning Low-Acid Foods

Low-acid foods are the heartier, less tangy counterparts in the world of canning. These include vegetables, meat, poultry, and seafood, among others. While they might not have the zingy acidity of high-acid foods, their higher pH level (above 4.6) presents a unique challenge in the canning process.

1. The pH level game

You see, the pH level acts as a crucial player in canning safety. The pH scale, which ranges from 0 to 14, measures the acidity or alkalinity of a substance. When a food's pH is below 4.6, it's considered high acid and safer for water bath canning. However, low-acid foods, with a pH above 4.6, create a more welcoming environment for the growth of harmful microorganisms.

2. Clostridium botulinum and the danger zone

Here's where the notorious guest of honor, Clostridium botulinum, enters the scene. This bacterium is a major concern in low-acid canning because it thrives in less acidic environments. It's the same microorganism responsible for botulism, a potentially life-threatening foodborne illness.

3. Pressure canners to the rescue

So, how do you safely can low-acid foods like vegetables, meats, and poultry? The solution lies in a handy kitchen companion: the pressure canner. Unlike water bath canning, pressure canning achieves the high temperatures necessary to neutralize any lurking Clostridium botulinum spores. The combination of elevated heat and pressure is the tag team that ensures these potential spoilers are effectively dealt with.

In this high-temperature environment, you can confidently preserve your low-acid foods, knowing that they'll be safe for long-term storage. By following the proper guidelines and using a pressure canner, you'll successfully unlock the world of delicious, low-acid canned creations while keeping your culinary adventures risk-free.

Acidified Foods and Formulated Acid Foods

In our journey to understand the ins and outs of canning, let's shed some light on two essential categories beyond the realm of high-acid and low-acid foods.

Acidified Foods

The key concept with acidified foods is the addition of an acid, typically vinegar or lemon juice, to the food product. This acid infusion lowers the food's pH level, making it acidic and safe for water bath canning. The recommended pH level for these foods is generally below 4.6.

Acidified foods include various pickled items, such as cucumbers, peppers, and relishes. These are often prepared by immersing the vegetables in a brine solution that contains vinegar or lemon juice.

It's crucial to ensure that the acid is added in the right proportion as specified in tested canning recipes. An incorrect acid-to-food ratio can lead to an unsafe pH level, compromising the preservation's safety.

Formulated Acid Foods

In the case of formulated acid foods, the pH level is intentionally adjusted to a safe range by adding acids or buffers. This is often done in recipes to ensure that the final product has the necessary acidity for canning.

Formulated acid foods might include tomato-based products like spaghetti sauce or salsa, where citric acid or lemon juice is added to maintain the required acidity.

Following canning recipes meticulously is essential for formulated acid foods. Deviating from the recipe's acid adjustments can alter the pH level and compromise the safety of the canned product.

There are a few common considerations you need to keep in mind when it comes to acidified and formulated acid foods:

- Tested recipes

  - Whether you're working with acidified or formulated acid foods, using tested canning recipes is a must. These recipes have undergone rigorous evaluation to ensure they meet safety standards.

- Proper measurements

  - Accurate measurement of acids and pH is vital. Investing in a pH meter or pH test strips can be useful in ensuring precision.

- Record keeping

  - Keeping records of the canning process, including the type and quantity of acid used, is essential for troubleshooting or adjustment in case of issues.

Understanding acidified and formulated acid foods is fundamental in canning, as it determines the safety of your preserved goods. Following trusted recipes and paying close attention to the pH levels will help you create delicious, risk-free canned products that you can enjoy with confidence.

WHAT'S YOUR FLAVOR?

When we talk about canning and the role of acidity, it's not only about safety; it's also about flavor. The acids commonly used for food preservation—such as vinegar, lemon juice, and citric acid—play a vital role in making your canned goods not only safe but also delicious.

1. Vinegar

Vinegar is a versatile acid commonly used in canning. It's a product of fermented ethanol and offers both preservation and flavor-enhancing qualities. Depending on the type of vinegar used, it can add a distinct tangy flavor that complements various high-acid foods, such as pickles and some chutneys. The choice of vinegar can also influence the overall flavor profile of your canned items.

2. Lemon juice

Lemon juice is another popular acid for canning. It brings a refreshing citrusy flavor to preserved foods, particularly those where a zesty, bright note complements the natural taste of the ingredients. Lemon juice serves the dual purpose of adding taste and acting as an effective preservative.

3. Citric acid

Citric acid, a natural acid found in citrus fruits like lemons and limes, is often used in canning for its ability to adjust acidity levels. Unlike vinegar and lemon juice, citric acid is flavor-neutral, meaning it won't overpower the taste of the food it preserves. It's primarily used to ensure the safety of the product without significantly altering its taste.

Acidity isn't just about preserving food; it's about elevating its taste. The addition of acid in canning recipes can transform the flavor profile of your preserved items. The following are some key ways in which acidity can enhance the taste of your canned goods:

1. Depth

Acidity contributes depth to dishes. It enhances the overall flavor, making it more complex and interesting. For instance, the tangy notes from vinegar or lemon juice can brighten and intensify the taste of canned goods, creating a more satisfying and enjoyable culinary experience.

2. Counteracting bitterness

Acids have the remarkable ability to counteract bitterness in certain foods. They can naturally balance and mellow out bitter flavors, making your preserved creations more palatable. For example, in pickling, the tang of vinegar can offset the natural bitterness of cucumbers.

3. Complementing other tastes

Acids play a vital role in the world of taste. They represent one of the five basic tastes humans can experience (sweet, sour, salty, bitter, and umami). The sourness they bring to the table complements the other taste sensations, adding harmony and balance to your dishes.

In essence, the judicious use of acidity in canning not only ensures the safety and preservation of your foods but also adds a layer of complexity and vibrancy to their flavor. The next time you enjoy a can of homemade pickles, a jar of fruit preserves, or a bowl of zesty salsa, remember that it's the well-balanced acidity that not only keeps them safe but also makes them a true culinary delight.

GETTING IT JUST RIGHT: TESTING FOOD ACIDITY

Testing the acidity of your foods is a fundamental step in ensuring that your canning adventures are not only safe but also result in flavors that delight your taste buds. This section will guide you through the process of testing the acidity of your foods, allowing you to make informed decisions about which canning method to employ.

Methods for Testing Acidity

pH Meter

A pH meter is a sophisticated and precise tool commonly used in laboratories, food processing, and canning to measure the acidity of substances. It provides a digital reading of the pH level, which is an efficient way to determine whether your food falls into the high-acid or low-acid category.

Let's have a look at how a pH meter works.

- **Precision**

  - pH meters are highly accurate and provide a precise pH value for your food. This is essential in canning, as it ensures that you have an exact measurement to make informed decisions about the canning method to use.

- **Calibration**

  - Before use, pH meters need to be calibrated according to the manufacturer's instructions. Calibration is the process of setting the meter to a known standard, ensuring the accuracy of the readings. The standard solutions used for calibration have a defined pH value.

- **Measurement**

  - Once calibrated, the pH meter's electrode is inserted into your food sample. The meter measures the hydrogen ion concentration in the sample and provides a digital reading. This reading allows you to accurately determine whether your food is high acid or low acid.

- **Accuracy**

  - pH meters are especially useful when you require high accuracy, such as when canning large batches of food. They offer a level of precision that can be crucial in preserving the safety and flavor of your canned goods.

Paper pH Strips

Paper pH strips are a cost-effective and user-friendly alternative to pH meters for testing acidity in foods.

- **Affordability**

  - Paper pH strips are budget-friendly and readily available in stores that carry canning supplies. They are a practical choice for home canners who may not require the precision of a pH meter.

- **Dip and compare**

  - To use paper pH strips, take a representative sample of your food and ensure it's well-mixed. Then, simply dip a paper pH strip into the food or liquid. You'll need to wait for the specified time mentioned in the instructions for the strip you're using.

- **Color change**

  - After the waiting period, the pH strip undergoes a

color change. The strip's color corresponds to the pH level of the food. You can compare this color to a pH chart provided with the strips to determine the approximate pH level.

- **Estimation**

  - Paper pH strips provide a reasonable estimate of the pH level of your food. While they may not offer the precision of a pH meter, they can still help you make informed decisions about whether your food is high acid or low acid.

pH meters are highly accurate and provide a precise pH value, making them ideal for professional or large-scale canning operations. Paper pH strips are more budget-friendly and accessible for home canners and can provide a reasonable estimate of food acidity. Both methods are valuable tools in the canning process, allowing you to choose the appropriate canning method for your specific food items, ensuring both safety and flavor in your canned goods.

How to Test the pH

1. Preparing your sample

A. Gather a representative sample of the food you wish to test. Ensure that this sample is well-mixed, as this will provide a more accurate reading of the food's overall pH level.

B. Take a small portion of the sample, typically a few tablespoons, and place it in a clean and sanitized container. It's essential to work with a clean sample to avoid any contamination.

C. The quality of your sample is crucial because it represents the entire batch of food you plan to can. Make sure it is a fair and balanced representation.

2. Using a pH meter

A. Before using a pH meter, ensure that it is clean, calibrated, and in proper working condition. Calibration is vital for accurate results, as it sets the meter to a known standard.

B. Insert the pH meter's electrode into the prepared food sample, following the manufacturer's instructions. The electrode measures the concentration of hydrogen ions (acidity) in the food.

C. The pH meter will provide a digital reading that represents the pH level of your food sample. This reading is typically a number on the pH scale, which ranges from 0 (very acidic) to 14 (very alkaline). For canning purposes, focus on whether the pH is below 4.6 (high acid) or above 4.6 (low acid).

D. Ensure that you clean and calibrate the pH meter before each use to maintain its accuracy.

3. Using paper pH strips

A. Take a clean and sanitized container and pour a small

amount of your food sample into it. This will be the solution you'll use for testing with the pH strips.

B. Take one paper pH strip and dip it into the food sample. Be sure to immerse it fully and hold it in the food for the specified time mentioned in the instructions provided with the strips.

C. After the waiting period, remove the pH strip and observe the color change. Different strips may have varying color charts, so refer to the one that came with your strips.

D. Compare the color on the pH strip to the color chart to determine the approximate pH level of your food sample. Note the pH level that corresponds to the closest color match.

Accurate pH testing is a critical aspect of the canning process, as it guides you in choosing the appropriate preservation method. If your food measures below 4.6 on the pH scale, it falls into the high-acid category suitable for water bath canning. If it measures above 4.6, it's considered low acid and should be preserved using a pressure canner to ensure both safety and flavor in your canned goods.

In the next chapter, "Wholesome Food," we'll delve into the significance of using quality ingredients in your canning adventures. Understanding the importance of the ingredients you choose will not only result in safer and healthier canned goods but also elevate the overall taste and satisfaction of your culinary creations. So, let's continue our journey toward becoming proficient home canners.

3

WHOLESOME FOOD

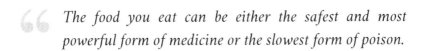 *The food you eat can be either the safest and most powerful form of medicine or the slowest form of poison.*

— ANN WIGMORE

C anning isn't only about long-term food preservation; it's also about preserving the nutritional content of your foods. One of the significant advantages of canning is the ability to lock in the freshness and nutritional value of produce at its peak. Fresh fruits and vegetables are rich in vitamins, minerals, and antioxidants that support our immune system and overall health. However, these essential nutrients can degrade over time due to exposure to air, light, and heat.

CAN-DO MODEL: NUTRITION—PRESERVING THE GOODNESS

Canning acts as a guardian of the nutritional gold present in your foods. It's not just about long-term preservation; it's about sealing in the freshness and nutritional value of your produce when it's at its peak. When you can fruits and vegetables, you're essentially "locking in" these essential nutrients. Even months after the canning process, the vitamins and minerals within your preserved foods remain intact. This means you can tap into the goodness of your harvest whenever you need it—be it for a quick and nutritious meal or during times when fresh produce isn't readily available.

Canning goes beyond convenience; it offers an array of health benefits.

1. Nutrient retention

One of the primary advantages of canning is the ability to maintain the integrity of essential nutrients within the foods you preserve. When you can fruits and vegetables, you're essentially freezing their nutritional profiles at the moment of canning. This means that even months after the canning process, the vitamins and minerals within your preserved foods remain intact. For instance, vitamin C, a fragile and water-soluble nutrient, is known to be preserved well in canned fruits and vegetables.

2. Year-round access

Canning opens the door to year-round access to vital nutrients. With canned goods on your pantry shelves, you're no longer limited to specific seasons when certain fruits and vegetables are abundant. This constant supply of essential nutrients enhances your ability to maintain a balanced and nutritious diet throughout the year.

3. Reduction in food waste

Food waste is a significant global concern, and canning is a powerful tool in combating this issue. When you can your produce, you effectively extend its shelf life. This means you can enjoy the fruits of your labor before they go bad. By reducing food waste through canning, you not only benefit your nutrition but also contribute to the broader goal of sustainability.

4. Cost-effective nutrition

Canning can be a cost-effective way to access highly nutritious foods. Buying fresh produce in bulk during the peak of the harvest season and canning it for later use is often more economical than purchasing ready-made canned products. This cost-effectiveness is a significant advantage for individuals and families seeking to maintain a nutritious diet while managing their food budget.

While canning inherently preserves nutrients, there are ways to maximize the nutritional value of your canned goods.

1. Freshness matters

It's essential to start with the freshest and highest quality produce when canning. The nutrients in the ingredients you use directly impact the nutritional value of the final product. Opt for produce that is at its peak of ripeness and flavor.

2. Proper canning techniques

Following safe canning practices is crucial to ensure the highest nutrient retention. Avoid under-processing or over-processing, as it can affect the vitamins and minerals in your canned foods. Proper heating and sealing procedures are critical to maintain nutritional content.

3. Mindful preparation

Some nutrients are concentrated in or just beneath the skin of fruits and vegetables. Be mindful when peeling, trimming, or processing your produce. Minimize nutrient loss by preserving as much of the edible portions as possible.

As you delve into the world of canning and discover the wholesome benefits it offers, you'll come to appreciate not only the convenience of preserved foods but also their power to serve as a potent form of nourishment. Every jar you open represents a powerful source of essential vitamins, minerals, and antioxidants that can contribute to your well-being. The CAN-DO Model reminds us that the food we eat can be a potent form of medicine, safeguarding our health and vitality.

In the following sections, we'll explore techniques and tips to maximize the nutritional value of your canned goods, ensuring that every jar you open is a testament to the idea that the food you eat can be a powerful form of medicine.

FRESH VS. PRESERVED: A NUTRITIONAL SHOWDOWN

The nutritional debate between fresh foods and their canned counterparts has been a subject of much discussion. Let's delve deeper into this showdown and compare the nutrient retention of fresh foods versus their canned versions, shedding light on the surprising benefits that canning can offer in preserving essential nutrients.

Fresh foods are celebrated for their nutritional richness, and rightfully so. However, it's important to recognize that the clock starts ticking on their nutrient levels the moment they're harvested. Several factors contribute to the gradual breakdown of these essential vitamins and minerals. Once fruits and vegetables are harvested, they immediately begin to lose vitamins. This natural process is accelerated for some items, which means that within a few days, a significant portion of the vitamins may be gone.

Even storing produce in a refrigerator doesn't entirely halt this process. Even with refrigeration, a considerable portion of the vitamins may deteriorate within a week or two. This means that by the time you consume fresh produce, its nutritional content may have significantly diminished. This time-sensitive decline in nutrients underscores the challenges of relying solely on fresh foods for optimal nutrition.

This highlights a key advantage of canning: It helps preserve these essential nutrients, effectively locking in their goodness at the moment of canning. The result is that when you open a can of preserved food, you're accessing the same nutritional value the produce had when it was canned, regardless of the passage of time.

Contrary to common misconceptions, the canning process is not just about maintaining but can also enhance the nutritional value of foods. This is particularly true for some specific foods.

For example, some foods release more antioxidants when they're heated during the canning process. A prime example of this phenomenon is tomatoes and corn. Canning can actually elevate the antioxidant content in these foods. As a result, the canned versions can be richer in antioxidants compared to their fresh counterparts. This is a remarkable benefit of canning that often goes unnoticed.

Let's explore some comparison examples of fresh versus canned food to understand how canning can preserve and sometimes even enhance nutritional value.

1. Tomatoes

Fresh: Fresh tomatoes are a fantastic source of vitamins like vitamin C and antioxidants like lycopene. However, their nutritional content can decline over time, especially if they're not consumed shortly after harvesting.

Canned: Canned tomatoes can be richer in antioxidants, particularly lycopene, due to the heating process during canning. This means that you can enjoy a higher concentration of certain beneficial compounds in canned tomatoes.

2. Corn

Fresh: Fresh corn is a delightful summer treat, rich in fiber and vitamins. However, corn's natural sugars begin to convert to starch after harvest, potentially affecting its sweetness and nutritional content.

Canned: Canned corn, when properly processed, can retain its natural sweetness and nutritional value, making it a convenient and nutritious addition to your meals.

3. Peaches

Fresh: Fresh peaches are known for their vitamins, especially vitamin C, and fiber content. However, their delicate nature makes them prone to bruising and spoilage, limiting their shelf life.

Canned: Canned peaches, if prepared correctly, can preserve the fruit's vitamins and sweetness. They offer a longer shelf life and can be enjoyed well beyond peach season.

4. Green beans

Fresh: Fresh green beans are a good source of vitamins, including vitamin C and vitamin K. However, they can lose their crispness and nutritional value over time, especially if not stored properly.

Canned: Canned green beans can maintain their firm texture and nutritional content, providing a convenient and accessible source of vitamins and fiber year-round.

5. Spinach

Fresh: Fresh spinach is packed with essential nutrients like iron, vitamin K, and folate. However, its shelf life is relatively short, and nutrient loss can occur as it wilts.

Canned: Canned spinach can maintain its nutritional value and is an excellent option for adding greens to your meals, even when fresh spinach is not readily available.

These examples illustrate that while fresh foods are undeniably nutritious and delicious, canning offers a valuable alternative for preserving and sometimes even enhancing the nutritional content of certain foods. Canned goods provide year-round access to essential nutrients, minimize food waste, and are often more cost-effective. When considering the nutrition of your meals, don't overlook the benefits that canned foods can bring to your table.

A comprehensive study revealed some astonishing findings. Individuals who regularly consumed six or more canned items per week had higher intakes of 17 essential nutrients when compared to those who ate two or fewer canned items per week. This indicates that canned foods not only maintain their nutritional value but, in some instances, can even enhance it. The study underlines the fact that canned goods are not just a convenient pantry staple but a source of significant nutrition (McDonell, 2019).

As you explore the world of canning, you'll realize that it's not just about food preservation; it's about retaining and sometimes even improving the nutritional richness of your meals. Whether you're enjoying canned tomatoes in a hearty winter stew or savoring canned peaches in your morning yogurt, you're tapping into the power of canning to elevate every meal as a nutritional triumph. The showdown between fresh and canned foods reveals that canned goods have much to offer in terms of nutrition, making them a valuable addition to your culinary repertoire.

MAXIMIZING THE GOODNESS: TIPS FOR NUTRIENT-PACKED CANNED FOODS

Now that we understand that canning is about more than preservation, let's explore some practical tips to help you maximize the nutritional goodness of your canned creations. These tips will ensure that every jar you open is a treasure trove of essential nutrients.

1. Starting with fresh produce

Selecting fresh, ripe produce is the first step to nutrient-packed canned goods. Fresh fruits and vegetables, at their peak of ripeness, contain higher levels of vitamins, minerals, and antioxidants. Choosing top-quality ingredients ensures that your canned goods begin with the maximum nutritional potential.

2. The power of blanching

Blanching plays a crucial role in nutrient preservation during the canning process. This quick blanching step involves immersing vegetables in boiling water for a short time and then rapidly cooling them. It serves two key purposes: It inactivates enzymes that can break down nutrients, and it helps maintain the color and texture of the vegetables. Proper blanching ensures that the vegetables you can are not only visually appealing but also retain their nutritional value.

3. Adhering to processing times

Following the recommended processing times for each specific food is paramount. Overcooking can lead to significant nutrient loss. These processing times are carefully determined to strike a balance between ensuring food safety and preserving the nutritional content of the canned goods. When you follow these guidelines, you not only guarantee safe consumption but also nutrient-rich meals for your family.

4. Managing canning liquid

The canning liquid is an important factor in nutrient retention. To minimize the loss of water-soluble nutrients, such as vitamins and some minerals, use as little liquid as necessary when preparing your canned goods. By doing so, you ensure that these essential nutrients stay within the food, rather than leach into the canning liquid. Additionally, using flavorful liquids, like homemade broth or juices, can enhance the taste of your canned foods while maintaining their nutritional value.

5. High-quality jars and lids

The choice of jars and lids is not only about convenience but also about maintaining the nutritional goodness of your canned foods. High-quality jars and well-sealing lids prevent air from entering the jars, which can lead to nutrient degradation. Investing in durable jars and ensuring tight seals preserves the nutritional value of your canned goods over time.

6. Careful storage

Proper storage is the final piece of the puzzle in maintaining the nutritional content of your canned goods. A cool, clean, dark, and dry storage environment is essential. Exposure to light and heat can lead to the degradation of certain vitamins, such as vitamin C. A well-organized storage area ensures that your canned foods retain their nutrient content and remain safe and delicious for years to come.

These tips highlight the importance of attention to detail in every step of the canning process, from ingredient selection to storage. When you follow these guidelines, your commitment to preserving nutrients ensures that every jar you open is a source of health and vitality for your loved ones. Your dedication to maximizing the nutritional value of your canned goods elevates them from mere pantry staples to nutrient-packed culinary treasures.

Your efforts in canning are an investment in wholesome and nutritious meals for your family, offering both convenience and health benefits. In the next chapter, "Shelf Life," we'll delve into how to ensure the longevity of your canned culinary treasures, keeping them safe and delicious for years to come. So, let's continue our journey toward becoming proficient home canners while reaping the nutritional rewards.

4

SHELF LIFE

We've all experienced that moment of pantry exploration when we stumble upon a can of soup or a jar of cranberry sauce with an expiration date long past. The instinctive reaction is to consider discarding these items, fearing they may be unsafe to consume. However, here's a little-known fact: According to the USDA, shelf-stable foods are safe to eat indefinitely, even after their expiration dates have passed. So, what exactly do these dates signify if they don't necessarily indicate spoilage or safety concerns?

In the realm of canned goods, those stamped-on dates carry unique significance. While many dates on foods primarily relate to quality rather than safety, home canning provides you with an exceptional advantage. It allows you to take charge of the longevity and safety of your preserved foods in ways that store-bought items cannot match.

In the following sections, we'll delve into the shelf life of home-canned goods, exploring the factors that influence them and how you can maximize the lifespan of your culinary treasures while ensuring their safety and deliciousness.

CAN-DO MODEL: DURABILITY—ENSURING LONGEVITY OF CANNED GOODS

Home canning is not just about preserving your favorite foods; it empowers you to extend their shelf life well beyond those ambiguous "Best If Used By" dates while ensuring they maintain their quality and flavor. In this chapter, we'll delve into the factors that contribute to the longevity of canned products and explore best practices for storing these culinary treasures. You'll discover how to recognize signs of spoilage and, most importantly, how to ensure your preserves stand the test of time.

Remember, you're not just preserving food; you're preserving the assurance of delicious, safe, and wholesome meals for years to come.

Storing With Care

Now that we've established the extended shelf life and safety of home-canned goods, let's focus on one of the key components that contribute to this longevity: proper storage. Just like a fine wine, your canned products deserve a suitable environment to maintain their quality.

1. Light

Light exposure can adversely affect the quality and nutrient content of canned foods. Ultraviolet (UV) rays from sunlight can lead to flavor changes and nutrient degradation. To protect your canned goods, store them in a place where they are shielded from light. Dark storage areas like basements or pantries are ideal choices.

2. Heat

Elevated temperatures can cause unwanted changes in flavor, texture, and color in your canned goods. Extreme heat may even lead to spoilage. To ensure the longevity of your preserved foods, store them in a cool environment. Avoid keeping them in areas that are prone to temperature fluctuations, like a hot attic or a shelf exposed to direct sunlight.

3. Moisture

Although canned goods are sealed to keep moisture out, the surrounding environment can still impact the integrity of the seal, leading to potential spoilage. Ensure that the storage area is dry and well-ventilated to prevent the rusting of jar lids, which could compromise the quality of your canned goods.

4. Chipped jars

Any chipping or damage to the canning jars can compromise the seal and expose the contents to external elements. Inspect your jars before storing them to ensure there are no visible defects. Check the lids to make sure they are in good condition and have a proper seal. Properly sealed jars are essential for maintaining the quality and safety of your preserved foods.

By adhering to these storage guidelines and protecting your canned goods from light, heat, moisture, and physical damage, you can maximize their shelf life and maintain their quality for years to come. Proper storage practices are essential for preserving the integrity of your home-canned treasures.

Here are some key tips to help ensure the longevity and quality of your home-canned foods:

1. Ideal storage conditions

To maximize the shelf life of your canned goods, store them in a cool, dark, dry, and relatively stable environment. Your basement, pantry, or dedicated storage area are excellent options. Consistent temperatures throughout the year are crucial, so avoid locations with temperature fluctuations or excessive heat, such as attics or garages.

2. Labeling and dating

Labeling your canned goods is essential for proper organization and ensuring that you consume your preserved items in the correct order. Including the name of the food product and the month and year it was canned on each jar allows you to practice the first-in, first-out (FIFO) method, ensuring that you consume the oldest items first. This organized approach prevents items from languishing in storage beyond their peak quality.

By following these tips and storing your canned goods in an environment that shields them from light, heat, and excess moisture, you can significantly extend their shelf life. Proper storage and labeling practices are your allies in maintaining the freshness and quality of your culinary creations, allowing you to enjoy them for years to come. In the next section, we'll delve into how to recognize the signs of spoilage, an essential skill for ensuring the safety and enjoyment of your home-canned goods.

Recognizing Signs of Spoilage in Canned Goods

Ensuring the safety of your canned goods is paramount, and being able to identify signs of spoilage is a crucial skill for any home canner. Here, we will guide you through recognizing the telltale indicators that your canned foods may have spoiled and the importance of heeding these warnings to protect your health.

Mold

Mold growth on the surface of canned food is a clear indicator of spoilage. It appears as fuzzy, discolored patches and can vary in color. Mold growth occurs when food is improperly sealed or processed. It can happen if there is a breach in the jar's seal or if the food's pH level is too high, creating an environment conducive to mold growth.

Signs to look out for: Look for fuzzy, discolored patches on the surface of the food, which can vary in color.

What to do: Discard the entire contents of the jar, including any food touching the mold, as it may have invisible spores. Clean and sterilize the jar for future use.

How to avoid: Ensure a proper seal during canning and adhere to recommended canning methods. Use high-acid ingredients for canning or adjust the acidity level when necessary.

Scum or Film

Sometimes, there can also be a slimy or cloudy film that may form on the surface of canned goods. The formation of a slimy or cloudy film on canned food can result from bacterial contamination during the canning process.

- Signs to look out for: Watch for a slimy or cloudy film on the surface of the canned food.
- What to do: Discard the entire contents of the jar. Properly clean and sterilize the jar for future use.
- How to avoid: Follow strict hygiene and sanitation practices during canning. Ensure that the food is free from contamination, and use clean equipment and utensils.

Unnatural Colors or Textures

If the color of the food appears different from what you would expect or if there are uneven color changes, it's a sign of spoilage. For example, canned vegetables may turn brown or gray. Canned foods should maintain their expected textures. If the texture is slimy, excessively soft, or grainy, it can indicate spoilage.

Discoloration and changes in texture occur due to the breakdown of food components. Enzymatic reactions, exposure to excessive heat, or poor canning practices can lead to these changes.

- Signs to look out for: Watch for food that appears discolored or has an unnatural texture, such as slimy, excessively soft, or grainy.
- What to do: Discard the contents if there are significant changes in color or texture that are not typical for the canned product.
- How to avoid: Follow recommended canning methods and processing times. Use high-quality, fresh ingredients and avoid overcooking or overheating during canning.

Bulging Lids

When the lid of a canned jar is visibly bulging or appears convex, it suggests that the seal has been compromised. This is often caused by gas production within the jar due to microbial activity. The food from such jars should not be consumed.

Bulging lids indicate gas production inside the jar due to microbial activity. This can result from improper sealing, bacterial contamination, or inadequate heat treatment.

- Signs to look out for: Watch for lids that are visibly bulging or appear convex.
- What to do: Do not consume any contents from a jar with a bulging lid. Treat it as a potential health risk.
- How to avoid: Ensure proper sealing and adhere to recommended canning processes to prevent gas buildup. Store jars in cool, stable conditions.

Spurting Liquid When Opened

Upon opening a canned jar, if liquid spurts out forcefully or bubbles up, it indicates the presence of gas buildup within the jar. This gas production is a sign of spoilage. The contents should not be consumed.

Liquid spurting or bubbling indicates the presence of gas within the jar, resulting from microbial activity or inadequate heat processing.

- Signs to look out for: When the jar is opened, liquid spurts out forcefully or bubbles up.
- What to do: Do not consume any contents if liquid spurts or bubbles when the jar is opened.
- How to avoid: Properly seal jars and process them at the correct temperature and time. Ensure the food is free from contamination before canning.

Active Bubbling

Sometimes, canned goods may exhibit active bubbling even without being opened. This is due to the buildup of gas pressure inside the jar. The pressure increase is a clear sign of spoilage, and the food inside should not be consumed.

Active bubbling inside a sealed jar is a sign of gas pressure buildup, often caused by microbial activity, incomplete heat processing, or inadequate sealing.

- Signs to look out for: Watch for bubbling within the sealed jar, even without opening it.
- What to do: Do not consume any contents from a jar exhibiting active bubbling.
- How to avoid: Follow recommended canning procedures to ensure proper sealing and heat processing. Maintain sanitary conditions during canning to prevent microbial contamination.

Disagreeable, Off-Putting Odors

If you detect unpleasant or unusual odors when you open a canned jar, it's a significant red flag. Canned foods should typically have a neutral or familiar smell. Any disagreeable or off-putting odor indicates spoilage and makes the food unsafe to eat.

Unpleasant or unusual odors in canned food are a clear indication of spoilage. This odor can be caused by microbial contamination or chemical reactions within the jar.

- Signs to look out for: When you open a canned jar, if you detect an unusual or disagreeable odor that is not consistent with the food's typical smell, it's a sign of spoilage.
- What to do: Do not consume any contents from a jar with an off-putting or disagreeable odor. Consider it unsafe for consumption and discard it.
- How to avoid: Prioritize cleanliness and hygiene during the canning process to prevent microbial contamination. Follow recommended canning practices, including sealing and processing, to ensure the food's safety and quality. Additionally, use fresh and high-quality ingredients for canning to minimize the risk of spoilage. Properly store your canned goods in suitable conditions to prevent chemical reactions that can lead to off-putting odors.

Recognizing these signs of spoilage is essential for your safety. If you have any doubts about the condition of your canned goods, it's always best to err on the side of caution. Discard any items that display these spoilage indicators. Your health is not worth the risk, and proper disposal is the safest course of action. It's always better to be safe than sorry when it comes to canned food safety.

SEALED FOR FRESHNESS: THE KEY TO DURABILITY AND SAFETY OF CANNED GOODS

Seals and lids are often underappreciated components in the world of home canning, yet they play a pivotal role in maintaining the quality, safety, and extended shelf life of your home-canned goods. Their importance goes beyond being mere technical parts of the canning process; they are the unsung heroes that safeguard your culinary creations and ensure the quality, safety, and longevity of your canned goods.

1. Quality

Seals and lids are the guardians of the quality of your canned goods. They ensure that the flavors, textures, and overall characteristics of your provisions remain intact. The integrity of the seal preserves the food's sensory qualities, so when you open a jar, you can savor the same delightful taste and texture as when it was freshly canned.

2. Safety

Beyond quality, seals and lids are crucial for ensuring the safety of your home-canned foods. They create a hermetic seal that acts as a barrier to potential contaminants. Harmful microorganisms, such as bacteria and molds, rely on air and external elements to thrive. An airtight seal prevents these intruders from entering the jar and compromising the safety of your preserved foods. This is especially important when canning low-acid foods, which are more susceptible to botulism and other foodborne illnesses.

3. Longevity

The longevity of your home-canned provisions is closely tied to the effectiveness of the seals and lids. A secure and airtight seal prevents the ingress of oxygen, which is a primary factor in food deterioration. Oxygen can lead to oxidation, spoilage, and the development of off-flavors. The presence of air can also encourage the growth of spoilage microorganisms. By creating a hermetic barrier, seals and lids significantly extend the shelf life of your home-canned goods, allowing you to enjoy their deliciousness for an extended period.

Creating an airtight barrier within the canning jar is the primary function of seals and lids in home canning. This airtight environment serves as a formidable defense against a range of external factors that can lead to spoilage and food deterioration.

One of the most critical roles of an airtight barrier is to shield your canned goods from exposure to air. Oxygen, found in the air, is a primary contributor to food degradation. It can lead to oxidation, which causes changes in flavor, color, and texture. Oxygen also promotes the growth of aerobic spoilage microorganisms, leading to spoilage and food safety concerns. By creating an airtight environment, seals and lids prevent the entry of oxygen, preserving the quality and safety of your canned foods.

An effective airtight barrier is essential in keeping harmful microorganisms, such as bacteria and molds, at bay. These microorganisms require oxygen to thrive and reproduce. An airtight seal impedes their access to the food inside the jar. This is particularly crucial when canning low-acid foods, which are more susceptible to the growth of Clostridium botulinum, the bacterium responsible for botulism. Without an airtight barrier, the risk of bacterial contamination and spoilage increases significantly.

Achieving a vacuum seal is a fundamental goal in home canning. The expulsion of air from the jar and the creation of a vacuum inside it are fundamental steps that contribute to the safety and durability of your home-canned foods.

The creation of a vacuum seal serves as a crucial safeguard against the growth of harmful microorganisms within the canned food. Harmful microorganisms, particularly bacteria, require an environment with oxygen to thrive. By expelling the air from the jar during the canning process, you create an environment in which these microorganisms cannot proliferate. This is essential for ensuring the safety of your home-canned provisions.

Beyond safety, a vacuum seal is also instrumental in preserving the quality of your canned goods. When oxygen is removed from the jar, the potential for oxidation and off-flavor development is significantly reduced. This means that the flavors, colors, and textures of your preserved foods remain closer to their original, freshly canned state.

A vacuum seal plays a pivotal role in extending the shelf life of your home-canned provisions. By removing oxygen, you inhibit the processes that lead to food deterioration. This is particularly important for maintaining the freshness and safety of your canned goods over an extended period.

Seals and lids in home canning are integral to preserving the quality, safety, and longevity of your provisions. They create airtight barriers and vacuum seals that safeguard your culinary creations from external elements and prevent the growth of harmful microorganisms. Achieving effective seals and vacuum seals is fundamental for the success of your home canning endeavors and the enjoyment of your canned goods.

Tips for Successful Sealing

Now, let's dive in and find out how you can obtain a quality seal each and every time you can.

Proper Canning Procedures

1. High-quality ingredients

Start with fresh, high-quality ingredients. The quality of the ingredients you use greatly affects the final product. Choose fruits and vegetables at their peak ripeness for maximum flavor and nutrient retention.

2. Appropriate equipment

Use canning equipment that is specifically designed for home canning. Ensure that your jars are in good condition without any chips or cracks. Replace jar lids and bands if they show signs of wear or damage.

3. Follow processing times

Adhere to the recommended processing times and methods for the specific food you are canning. These times are carefully calculated to ensure the safety and quality of the canned goods.

4. Sterile environment

Maintain a sterile environment by cleaning and sanitizing all equipment and work surfaces. This helps prevent contamination that could compromise the seals and the safety of your canned foods.

Testing the Seal

1. Popping sound

After removing the jars from the canner and as they begin to cool, listen for a distinctive popping sound. This sound is a reassuring confirmation that the vacuum seal has successfully formed. If you hear this sound, it's an excellent indicator that the contents are sealed properly.

2. Visual inspection

Besides the popping sound, visually inspect the lids. A properly sealed jar will have a slightly concave (indented) lid. This visual cue is another sign that the vacuum seal is intact.

What to Do If the Jar Is Not Sealed

If you discover that a jar has not been sealed properly, it's essential to take immediate action to prevent spoilage and ensure safety.

1. Isolation

Do not store unsealed jars with sealed ones. Unsealed jars are more susceptible to spoilage, and it's crucial to keep them separate.

2. Reprocessing

One option is to reprocess the food in a new jar. Follow proper canning procedures to ensure that a good seal is achieved during reprocessing. This may involve reheating the food and transferring it to a new jar with a fresh lid.

3. Refrigeration

If reprocessing is not possible or practical, promptly refrigerate the unsealed jar and consume its contents as soon as possible.

Refrigeration helps slow down any potential spoilage and ensures safety.

Mastering the art of seal integrity is a fundamental aspect of successful home canning. By following these tips and being attentive to proper procedures and the condition of your seals, you can consistently produce safe, high-quality, and long-lasting home-canned goods. This knowledge not only ensures the safety of your preserved foods but also opens the door to a satisfying and rewarding journey in the world of home canning.

MAKE A DIFFERENCE WITH YOUR REVIEW

Unlock the Magic of Canning and Food Preservation

"Preserving the past is a gift for the future."

— ANONYMOUS

People who share the sweetness of knowledge make the world a better place. So, in the spirit of preserving traditions and spreading the joy of homemade delights, let's embark on a journey together.

Would you share the secrets of a timeless tradition, even if you didn't get credit for it?

Who is this person you ask? They are like you. Or, at least, like you used to be. Eager to explore, wanting to make a difference, and needing guidance, but unsure where to find it.

My mission is to make the art of canning accessible to everyone. Everything I do stems from that mission. And the only way for us to accomplish that mission is by reaching... well... everyone.

This is where you come in. Most people do, in fact, judge a book by its cover (and its reviews). So here's my ask on behalf of someone discovering the wonders of canning for the first time:

Please help that budding canner by leaving a review for "Canning Mastery."

Your gift costs no money and less than 60 seconds to make real, but it can change a fellow canner's life forever. Your review could help...

...one more family savor the flavors of home.
...one more kitchen echo with laughter and stories.
...one more person discover the joy of tradition.
...one more heart connect with the simple pleasures.

To get that 'feel good' feeling and help this person for real, all you have to do is...and it takes less than 60 seconds... leave a review.

Simply scan the QR code below to leave your review:

If you feel good about sharing the warmth of tradition, you are my kind of person. Welcome to the club. You're one of us.

I'm that much more excited to share the magic of canning with you, to make your kitchen a place of joy and tradition. You'll love the techniques and flavors I'm about to share in the coming chapters.

Thank you from the bottom of my heart. Now, back to our regularly scheduled canning adventure.

Your biggest fan,
Caleb Quinn

PS - Fun fact: If you share something delightful with another person, it makes you more delightful to them. If you have a friend who loves the kitchen magic, and you believe this book will bring a smile to their face, send it their way.

5

SEAL THE DEAL

 By failing to prepare, you are preparing to fail.

— BENJAMIN FRANKLIN

The words of Benjamin Franklin ring true when it comes to canning, as planning and organizing are key steps to ensure safe and healthy canning. Organization is crucial in canning to ensure the safety of the food you're preserving. Having a structured and organized approach helps minimize the risk of errors that could lead to unsafe or spoiled canned goods. This is especially important in home canning, where the risk of botulism and other foodborne illnesses is a concern.

Being well-organized streamlines the canning process, making it more efficient. You'll spend less time searching for tools, ingredients, or recipes and more time focused on the canning steps themselves. This efficiency can make the canning experience more enjoyable and less stressful.

Well-organized canning ensures the quality of your preserved foods. This includes using proper equipment, following recommended procedures, and maintaining accurate records. Quality is vital to the long-term success of your home-canned goods.

In this chapter, we'll explore the key aspects of organization in home canning, starting with the essential tools and equipment required for a successful canning experience. These tools are your allies throughout the canning process and help maintain the quality and safety of your preserved foods.

By understanding the significance of organization in canning and following the guidelines in this chapter, you'll be well-prepared to embark on successful canning projects. Organization sets the foundation for safety, efficiency, and quality in your home canning endeavors, making it a key component of your journey to becoming a proficient home canner.

CAN-DO MODEL: ORGANIZATION—STREAMLINING THE PROCESS FOR SAFETY AND EFFICIENCY

The Canning Tool Kit

Let me introduce you to the must-have tools and equipment to ensure that you're well-prepared to embark on your canning journey. From the basics like jars, lids, and a cooker to more specialized items like a food mill or an immersion blender, you'll learn the purpose of each and why it's an essential part of your canning arsenal.

1. Canning jars and lids

A. Purpose: Jars and lids are the core vessels for preserving your canned goods. They come in various sizes, from half-pint to quart-sized jars, allowing you to store a wide range of foods.

B. Importance: Proper jars and lids are crucial for achieving a safe and airtight seal. The choice of jar size depends on the type of food you're preserving and the quantity you plan to store.

2. Jar lifter and lid lifter

A. Purpose: These specialized tools help you safely handle hot jars and lids during the canning process.

B. Importance: They prevent accidents, burns, and contamination by allowing you to lift hot jars and lids without direct contact, ensuring your safety and the integrity of your preserves.

3. Canning funnel

A. Purpose: A canning funnel is a funnel with a wide mouth that fits perfectly into canning jars, making it easier to fill the jars with your prepared foods without spilling or creating a mess.

B. Importance: It helps maintain the recommended

headspace (the space between the food and the jar's rim) for proper sealing and ensures a clean, spill-free filling process.

4. Ladle

A. Purpose: This tool is essential for transferring hot liquids, such as jams, sauces, soups, and pickling brines, into your canning jars with precision and minimal spillage.

B. Importance: A ladle ensures that you can pour hot liquids safely and efficiently, helping maintain the cleanliness of your canning process.

5. Bubble freer and headspace tool

A. Purpose: These tools help remove trapped air bubbles from your filled jars and measure the appropriate headspace, which is the gap between the food and the jar's rim. Proper headspace is crucial for achieving a successful seal.

B. Importance: Ensuring there are no air bubbles in your jars and maintaining the recommended headspace is vital for the canning process, as it affects the quality of the seal and the preservation of your food.

6. A cooker or canner

A. Purpose: The type of canner you choose depends on the foods you plan to preserve. For water bath canning, a water bath canner is suitable, while pressure canning requires a pressure canner to safely process low-acid foods.

B. Importance: Using the correct canner for the type of food you're preserving is essential for safety. The canner creates the necessary conditions for sealing and preserving your canned goods effectively.

7. Good kitchen towels

A. Purpose: Quality kitchen towels are used for keeping your workspace clean and dry, whether you're handling hot jars or preparing canning ingredients.

B. Importance: Kitchen towels help maintain a hygienic and organized workspace, preventing accidents, and contamination, and maintaining cleanliness throughout the canning process.

8. A home canning cookbook

A.Purpose: A comprehensive canning cookbook serves as your guide to tried-and-true recipes, techniques, and safety guidelines for successful home canning.

B. Importance: It's an essential resource for both beginners and experienced canners, providing reliable recipes, safety instructions, and troubleshooting tips to ensure your preserves are safe and delicious.

9. Additional kitchen tools

A. Purpose: Depending on the recipes you choose, you may find tools like a food mill or food strainer, immersion blender, apple peeler, multi-chopper, and labels handy for various canning projects.

B. Importance: These additional tools streamline specific canning tasks, such as pureeing, peeling, or chopping ingredients, and help with organization and clear jar identification.

10. Pantry ingredients

A. Purpose: Essential ingredients like pectin, lemon juice, vinegar, apple cider vinegar, and sugar or honey are often used in canning recipes to achieve the perfect taste, consistency, and preservation of your canned goods.

B. Importance: Having these pantry ingredients on hand ensures you can follow recipes accurately and achieve the desired results in your preserves.

Having the right tools at your disposal ensures that your canning process is efficient and safe, resulting in delicious and well-preserved foods that you can enjoy for months or even years. As you gather your canning tool kit, you'll be well-prepared to embark on your canning adventures. So, let's continue our journey to becoming proficient home canners and creating culinary delights that stand the test of time.

THE PERFECT CANNING SPACE

Creating a dedicated canning workspace is a game-changer for efficiency and safety. It allows you to streamline the process while ensuring that your canned goods are prepared and stored safely. Here, we'll look at guidance on setting up and organizing a canning workspace that maximizes efficiency without compromising safety.

Storage

A well-organized canning space begins with storage. Sturdy shelves or cabinets are essential for keeping your canning supplies and ingredients neatly organized and easily accessible. Consider clear, airtight containers for pantry staples like sugar, flour, or dried herbs, as they make it simple to see what you have and keep ingredients fresh.

Appliances

While traditional canning is often done on a stove-top, modern appliances can significantly enhance efficiency. Having a high-quality range for cooking and preparing ingredients is essential. Additionally, a pressure canner is a valuable tool for safely canning low-acid foods, as it uses pressure to ensure proper preservation. Some canners also use a second oven to keep jars and lids hot and sterilized until they're ready to be filled.

However, always ensure that your appliances are in excellent working condition and properly calibrated for canning purposes.

Counter Space

A clean and spacious countertop is a must for efficient canning. You need enough room for prepping ingredients, filling jars, and cooling freshly canned goods. Keeping your countertop clutter-free allows for a seamless workflow and ensures that you have the space needed for different tasks throughout the canning process.

Safety

While efficiency is essential, it should never compromise safety. Safety should be a top priority in your canning space. Ensure that your workspace adheres to safety guidelines. This includes having proper ventilation to help remove steam and odors generated during canning. Good lighting is crucial to avoid accidents and ensure you can work safely. Implement fire safety measures in your canning space to prevent accidents related to hot stoves and appliances. It's also vital to follow tested canning recipes and recommendations to the letter to guarantee the safety of your preserved foods, as deviating from these can lead to spoilage or even foodborne illnesses.

By creating a dedicated canning space that balances efficiency and safety, you'll not only enjoy the canning process more but also ensure that your culinary creations are of the highest quality and taste.

PLANNING FOR SAFETY

Canning is not only about preserving the deliciousness of your foods but also ensuring that your creations are safe for consumption. Let's discuss the safety precautions you should consider when canning at home to protect your health and that of your loved ones.

Foods You Should Never Can at Home

1. Dairy products

Dairy products such as milk, cheese, and butter can harbor harmful bacteria, including botulism. Canning cannot reach the high temperatures required to make dairy safe, and the risk of spoilage is high.

2. Lard

Lard is a type of fat that can turn rancid during the canning process due to prolonged storage. The process of canning doesn't preserve lard effectively.

3. Purees

Foods with a mashed or pureed consistency, such as baby foods or some sauces, can become too dense for safe canning. The density makes it challenging for heat to penetrate thoroughly, which may result in uneven processing.

4. Dry goods (flour, pasta, rice)

Dry goods like flour, pasta, and rice can absorb liquid during the canning process. This absorption can lead to spoilage or undesirable changes in texture. Canning is not suitable for preserving these types of items.

5. Cornstarch and arrowroot powder

These are thickening agents commonly used in cooking. When canned, they can result in inconsistent and unpredictable outcomes, making it difficult to achieve safe and reliable results.

6. Nut butters

Nut butters like peanut butter or almond butter have a dense consistency. This density can create issues during canning, making it challenging to achieve safe and consistent results. Additionally, oils in nut butter can separate and spoil.

Avoid These Dangerous Canning Methods

There's certainly a lot of information available on the internet about unconventional canning methods, and many may claim that these methods work and are safe. However, for various reasons, these methods should be avoided.

1. Slow cooker, dishwasher, microwave, and solar oven canning

These appliances are not designed for canning, and their temperatures may not reach or sustain the levels needed to destroy harmful microorganisms. Inconsistent temperatures can lead to underprocessing, allowing bacteria to survive and multiply.

The risk is much higher when using these devices for bacterial contamination and spoilage, posing health risks to consumers. The lack of proper sealing when using these devices may result in unsafe storage conditions.

2. Oven canning

Standard kitchen ovens are not reliable for canning because they lack the precise temperature control required. Heat distribution in ovens can vary, leading to unevenly processed jars.

The unreliable temperature control may result in underprocessed or overprocessed foods. Inadequate heat may not destroy bacteria, while excessive heat can cause overcooking and compromise food quality.

3. Open kettle canning

This method involves filling jars with hot food and sealing them without further processing. Without proper heat treatment and vacuum sealing, it fails to destroy harmful microorganisms and create a sterile environment for long-term storage.

Incomplete processing increases the risk of bacterial growth, spoilage, and the potential for unsafe canned goods. The absence of a vacuum seal may lead to contamination.

4. Inversion canning

Inversion canning involves flipping hot, filled jars upside down after sealing. This method doesn't guarantee a proper vacuum seal, and the cooling process may not create a secure seal.

Jars may not seal effectively, exposing the contents to air and contaminants. The lack of a proper seal increases the risk of spoilage, and the method is not recommended for ensuring safe preservation.

5. Using a water bath canner instead of a pressure canner for low-acid foods

Water bath canning is suitable only for high-acid foods due to its inability to reach the high temperatures required to eliminate harmful bacteria in low-acid foods. Low-acid foods need the specialized conditions provided by a pressure canner.

Inadequate processing temperatures can lead to the survival of bacteria like Clostridium botulinum, which can produce toxins causing botulism. Botulism is a severe and potentially fatal form of food poisoning.

It's crucial to use approved canning methods and equipment to ensure the safety of preserved foods. Always follow reliable recipes and guidelines from reputable sources to reduce the risk of foodborne illnesses associated with improper canning practices.

Changing and Adapting Canning Recipes Safely

Canning recipes are carefully designed to ensure the preservation and safety of the canned goods. Any changes that affect the acidity, density, or composition of the food can lead to unsafe or spoiled results. It's crucial to follow trusted and tested canning recipes closely. If you want to make significant modifications, it's advisable to find a recipe specifically designed for the ingredients and alterations you have in mind to ensure safety and quality.

1. Salt, seasonings, equivalent acids, and sugar

Adjusting the salt, seasonings, equivalent acids (such as lemon juice or vinegar), and sugar in a canning recipe is generally safe. These changes are primarily for flavor and can be customized to suit your preferences.

2. Adding ingredients

You can safely add certain ingredients like peppers, onions, herbs, and spices to canning recipes to enhance flavor. Ensure that the additional ingredients are also suitable for canning and do not significantly alter the overall acidity of the recipe.

3. Changing the ratio of low-acid to high-acid ingredients

One modification that should always be avoided is altering the ratio of low-acid to high-acid ingredients in a recipe meant for water bath canning. This is especially important when canning low-acid foods like vegetables, meats, and stews. If you adjust this ratio inappropriately, it can compromise the safety and quality of the final product.

Following these safety precautions is essential when it comes to home canning. It's crucial to be aware of which foods are safe for canning and which should be avoided, as well as the dangerous methods that should never be used for canning. Additionally, while making minor adjustments to canning recipes for personal taste is acceptable, it's important to avoid changes that could compromise the safety and quality of the final product. By prioritizing safety in your canning practices, you can enjoy the delicious and well-preserved foods you create.

ALL ABOUT LABELS

Properly labeling your canned goods is a crucial step in your canning journey. Not only does it help you identify what's in each jar, but it also ensures the safety and quality of your preserved foods.

1. Identification of contents

Purpose: Easily identify the type of food stored in each jar

Importance: Prevents confusion and ensures you can quickly locate specific items in your pantry

2. Tracking freshness

Purpose: Includes the month and year of canning on the label

Importance: Helps track the freshness of canned goods, allowing you to prioritize consumption based on canning dates

3. Efficient rotation

Purpose: Enables establishing an efficient rotation system

Importance: Ensures that older batches are used first, promoting a first-in, first-out (FIFO) approach to prevent items from expiring

4. Safety assurance

Purpose: Supports adherence to recommended consumption timelines

Importance: Prevents the consumption of foods past their safe storage duration, contributing to overall food safety

5. Organization in the pantry

Purpose: Aids in organizing your pantry effectively
Importance: Allows for a visually appealing and well-organized storage system, making it easy to manage inventory

6. Prevention of waste

Purpose: Facilitates monitoring and management of canned goods
Importance: Reduces the likelihood of forgotten or overlooked items, minimizing the risk of wastage

7. Quick recipe reference

Purpose: Simplifies meal planning and recipe selection
Importance: Enables you to easily identify available ingredients for cooking or baking without opening every jar

8. Quality control

Purpose: Helps monitor the quality of preserved foods
Importance: Allows you to visually inspect jars for signs of spoilage or issues, ensuring you consume safe and high-quality products

9. Customization and personalization

Purpose: Adds a personal touch to your home-canned goods

Importance: Enhances the overall experience of preserving foods and makes it a more enjoyable and personalized activity

10. Sharing or gifting

Purpose: Facilitates sharing or gifting of home-canned items

Importance: Clearly labeled jars make for thoughtful and personalized gifts, allowing recipients to appreciate the contents

Labeling is a simple yet essential practice in home canning that contributes to the safety, organization, and enjoyment of preserved foods. It ensures that your efforts in preserving the harvest result in a well-managed and accessible pantry. Here are some details that you can include on your canning labels:

1. Name of the food product: This is important as it helps you to easily identify the contents of each jar, which comes quite handy when you have a lot. For example, "Strawberry Jam," "Blueberry Preserves," or "Bread and Butter Pickles."
2. Month and year canned: This little detail enables you to keep track of the freshness of canned goods and helps you establish an efficient rotation system.

Labeling is a great way to stay organized, but it can come with its challenges. Here are some tips you can make use of to avoid and overcome labeling challenges:

- **Writing on lids:** When writing directly on lids, use a permanent marker and write clearly and legibly for easy identification.
- **Labeling jars with tattler lids:** Make use of labels that adhere securely or use markers directly on lids. Also, ensure labels or writing are moisture-resistant to prevent smudging.
- **Printing labels:** Consider printing labels using a label maker or computer. Choose label material suitable for canning to prevent deterioration.
- **Labeling multiple batches:** Use different colors or styles of labels for each batch. This enables you to quickly identify the vintage canned goods and use older batches first.
- **Using painter's tape labels:** Use painter's tape labels for temporary and easy removal. The tape is suitable for jars that may be repurposed frequently without leaving residue.
- **Pro tips:** Consider laminating handwritten labels or using waterproof markers for enhanced durability. Regularly check labels for any signs of wear or fading, especially in humid storage conditions.

Well-labeled jars contribute to an organized pantry, facilitating easy retrieval and inventory management. Knowing the canning date helps ensure that foods are consumed within recommended time frames, prioritizing both safety and quality.

By mastering the art of labeling, you not only enhance the visual appeal of your pantry but also contribute to the overall safety and enjoyment of your home-canned goods. Now, armed with this knowledge, let's continue our journey into the next chapter and continue making a splash in the world of home canning!

6

MAKING A SPLASH

 Canned tomatoes are like summer saved all that deep sun-kissed flavor ready to be enjoyed.

— BETTER HOMES AND GARDENS

Each jar of preserved food is indeed a cherished time capsule, a vibrant mosaic capturing the essence of seasons and cherished memories. Imagine the sun-kissed days of summer, the fields adorned with ripe, juicy tomatoes basking in the warmth of the sun. In that moment, nature's bounty is at its peak, flavors intensified by the sun and soil, memories made amid the harvest.

Canning these tomatoes is like bottling time itself. It's a meticulous craft, an art form that allows us to encapsulate the very best of nature's offerings. As each tomato is carefully prepared and preserved, it becomes more than just a piece of fruit; it transforms into a repository of summer's vitality, a testament to the sun-soaked days and the hard work of nurturing the land.

When you crack open a jar of canned tomatoes on a chilly winter day, you're met with an explosion of flavors and aromas, reminiscent of the sun-drenched afternoons and the laughter shared with loved ones while picking them. It's a taste of nostalgia, a reminder of the joy of harvest season and the anticipation of the months to come.

These preserved tomatoes are not simply culinary delights; they are stories preserved in glass. Each jar tells a tale of abundance, of the vibrant hues of summer, and the promise of hearty meals shared with family and friends. It's a way to bring back the taste of sunshine during the gloomy days, a reminder that nature's bounty, once captured, can continue to bring warmth and joy long after the harvest is over.

So, as you savor a spoonful of those canned tomatoes, remember that you're not just tasting a fruit—you're tasting a moment in time, a piece of summer saved, and a testament to the beauty of preserving nature's gifts. Each jar is a celebration of the seasons, a homage to the past, and an invitation to create new memories with every delicious bite.

WATER BATH CANNING

Water bath canning, often seen as an art form of preserving, is a technique that allows you to capture the essence of the seasons and preserve your favorite fruits and high-acid foods with precision. At its core, water bath canning is a method that relies on the application of heat to preserve foods by eliminating harmful microorganisms, particularly suited for high-acid foods. It's a practice deeply rooted in tradition and history, a technique passed down through generations of home canners. With water bath canning, you can bottle the flavors of the season and have them at your disposal year-round.

The science of canning revolves around temperature. Understanding how heat plays a crucial role in protecting your canned goods from spoilage is key. By subjecting jars filled with food and liquid to the right temperatures, you can inactivate enzymes, destroy harmful microorganisms, and create a hostile environment for spoilage agents.

Why Water Bathing Is Done

Water bath canning goes beyond preservation; it enhances the quality and shelf life of your canned goods. The high temperatures reached during the process not only kill off unwanted microorganisms but also help meld flavors and ensure the contents of your jars are safe to consume.

Emphasizing Key Considerations

Water bath canning isn't a one-size-fits-all solution. You need to recognize its limitations, establish a suitable setup, select the right jar sizes, and understand the importance of timing. This method is most suitable for high-acid foods such as tomatoes, fruits, and pickles, making it essential to grasp the finer details.

Your Altitude Matters

Your geographic location matters when water bath canning. Altitude can influence the processing times required to ensure safe preservation. You'll need to adjust the canning process to suit the specific altitude of your location, which we'll provide guidance on.

As you begin your water bath canning journey, remember that each jar you create is a time capsule, preserving the vibrancy of the seasons and the cherished moments associated with them. With each twist of the lid, you unlock a burst of summery goodness, a reminder of the past, and an invitation to enjoy the present.

IDEAL SELECTIONS FOR WATER BATH CANNING

Water bath canning is a versatile and accessible method for preserving high-acid foods, allowing you to capture the essence of different seasons and savor the vibrant flavors of your favorite fruits. To embark on a successful water bath canning journey, it's important to know which foods are suitable for this method and what you'll need to get started.

High-Acid Foods Suitable for Water Bath Canning

Tomatoes

Tomatoes are a favorite among water bath canners. They offer numerous culinary possibilities, from tomato sauce to whole peeled tomatoes. Their high acidity makes them an excellent candidate for water bath canning. You can create a variety of tomato-based products to enjoy throughout the year.

Fruits

High-acid fruits like berries, cherries, and peaches are perfect for water bath canning. These fruits not only meet the acidity requirement but also come in various delectable recipes, such as fruit preserves and pie fillings. Whether you prefer jams, jellies, or canned fruits, the water bath method is ideal for preserving these flavorful treats.

Fruit Preserves

Various fruits like apricots, plums, and figs can be turned into delicious fruit preserves through water bath canning. These preserves are versatile and can be used as toppings for desserts, paired with cheeses, or spread on sandwiches and toast.

Fruit Pie Fillings

Prepare and can fruit pie fillings using high-acid fruits such as cherries, apples, and blueberries. These fillings make it easy to whip up homemade pies and desserts any time of the year.

Fruit Salsas

Create vibrant and tangy fruit salsas using ingredients like mangoes, pineapples, and citrus fruits. Fruit salsas can be a delightful addition to grilled meats, tacos, and seafood dishes.

Fruit Compotes

Compotes made from high-acid fruits are perfect for water bath canning. They can be served as a simple dessert on their own, paired with yogurt, or drizzled over ice cream.

Fruit Chutneys

High-acid fruits like apples and cranberries can be used to make sweet and tangy fruit chutneys. These chutneys are excellent condiments that complement a variety of dishes, including roasted meats, sandwiches, and cheese platters.

Fruit Syrups

Make fruit syrups from fruits like raspberries, blackberries, and strawberries. These syrups can be used to flavor beverages, drizzle over pancakes or waffles, or add a fruity twist to cocktails.

Fruit Butter

Fruit butter is a smooth, spreadable condiment made from high-acid fruits like apples or pears. It is delicious when spread on bread or used as a topping for pancakes and oatmeal.

Fruit Sauces

High-acid fruit sauces, such as cranberry sauce or raspberry sauce, can be used as accompaniments to poultry and desserts and even as a glaze for grilled meats.

Pickled Vegetables

Vegetables like cucumbers, beets, and other pickled delights add a zesty touch to your pantry. They're not only tasty but also easy to can using the water bath method. Pickled vegetables can be enjoyed on their own, added to salads, or used as side dishes, providing a burst of flavor to your meals.

Jams and Jellies

Sweet spreads made from high-acid fruits like strawberries and apricots are delightful treats for breakfast or dessert. Water bath canning is an excellent way to preserve their delicious flavors, ensuring that you have homemade jams and jellies on hand for spreading on toast, pastries, or as accompaniments to various dishes.

Water bath canning is a versatile and accessible method that allows you to capture the essence of the seasons in your jars, preserving the vibrant flavors of your favorite high-acid foods. Whether you're a seasoned canner or new to the practice, these high-acid foods offer a wide range of options for creating homemade delights that you can enjoy throughout the year.

Water Bath Canning Limitations

While water bath canning is ideal for high-acid foods, it's important to understand its limitations. Water bath canning relies on the natural acidity of certain foods to prevent the growth of harmful bacteria. Foods with a pH level of 4.6 or lower are considered high-acid and are suitable for water bath canning. These foods have a natural protective barrier that helps to ensure their safety when preserved using this method.

Water bath canning is perfect for preserving high-acid foods such as fruits and high-acid vegetables. These foods naturally have a pH level below 4.6, which inhibits the growth of harmful microorganisms, including botulism spores.

Water bath canning typically reaches temperatures of 212° Fahrenheit (100° Celsius), which is sufficient for preserving high-acid foods. However, low-acid foods need higher temperatures, typically around 240° Fahrenheit (116° Celsius), to destroy harmful bacteria and spores effectively. Water bath canning cannot reach these temperatures, making it unsafe for low-acid foods.

To safely can low-acid foods, you'll need specialized equipment known as a pressure canner. A pressure canner can achieve the higher temperatures necessary to eliminate the risk of botulism and other pathogens in low-acid foods.

Unsuitable for Low-Acid Foods

The key limitation of water bath canning is that it's not safe for low-acid foods. Low-acid foods include vegetables like carrots, green beans, and peas, as well as meats, seafood, poultry, chili, and corn. These foods have a pH level above 4.6, which means they lack the natural acidity required to protect against harmful bacteria.

1. Low-acid vegetables

Various low-acid vegetables, such as green beans, carrots, peas, corn, and asparagus, require pressure canning for safe preservation. These vegetables have pH levels higher than 4.6 and can support the growth of harmful bacteria like Clostridium botulinum.

2. Meats

Meats like beef, pork, poultry, and venison are low-acid foods that demand pressure canning. The high temperatures attained in pressure canning ensure the destruction of potential pathogens and spores in the meat.

3. Seafood

Seafood, including fish and shellfish, is typically low in acidity and should be preserved with pressure canning. This method guarantees the elimination of harmful microorganisms and extends the shelf life of these products.

4. Soups and stews

Any recipe that combines low-acid vegetables or meats with broth or other liquid components should be pressure canned. This includes dishes like beef stew or chicken soup.

5. Chili

Chili is a popular dish that often contains beans, meat, and a tomato base, but the overall pH level may not be sufficiently low to guarantee safe preservation. Pressure canning is recommended for chili.

6. Salsas with low-acid ingredients

While some salsas with high-acid ingredients can be water bath canned, salsas containing low-acid ingredients like black beans, corn, or significant amounts of low-acid vegetables should be pressure canned.

7. Pasta sauces with low-acid ingredients

Pasta sauces that incorporate low-acid ingredients such as meat, mushrooms, or a variety of vegetables should be pressure canned for safety.

8. Milk and dairy products

Milk and dairy products are not suitable for canning, as canning cannot reach the high temperatures required to make dairy safe. Instead, consider alternative preservation methods like freezing or refrigeration.

9. Gravies

Gravy is another example of a low-acid product that should be preserved using pressure canning.

Understanding these limitations is essential to ensure the safety and quality of your canned goods. Always use the appropriate canning method based on the acidity of the food you're preserving. Water bath canning is perfect for high-acid foods, while low-acid foods should be preserved using pressure canning to prevent any safety concerns.

Before you embark on your water bath canning journey, make sure you have the right equipment and ingredients ready.

ESSENTIAL EQUIPMENT AND INGREDIENTS

Properly equipping yourself with the right tools and ingredients is essential for a successful water bath canning session.

1. Water bath canner

A water bath canner is a large pot with a fitted lid and a rack designed specifically for water bath canning. The rack helps keep the jars from touching the bottom of the pot and allows water to circulate around them. It's important for processing your jars safely.

2. Jars

You'll need glass canning jars in various sizes, such as quart, pint, or half-pint, depending on your recipes. Ensure the jars are free of cracks or defects, as any damage can lead to seal failure. Before using them, clean and sanitize the jars properly. You can sanitize them in your canner or dishwasher.

3. Lids and bands

Canning lids are essential for sealing your jars, and they come in various sizes that match the jar size you're using. Bands, also known as screw bands, secure the lids during processing. Lids are typically used only once, but bands can be reused as long as they are in good condition.

4. Fresh ingredients

Choose high-acid fruits or foods that are ideal for water bath canning. This includes items like tomatoes, berries, peaches, and pickled vegetables. Fresh, ripe produce will yield the best results.

5. Canning tools

Several canning tools can make your process smoother and safer.

- Jar lifter

This tool helps you lift hot jars in and out of the canner.

- Canning funnel

It makes filling jars with hot liquids cleaner and less wasteful.

- Headspace tool

This ensures you leave the correct amount of empty space (headspace) at the top of the jar, which is essential for proper sealing.

- Bubble remover

It helps release air bubbles trapped in the jar, which could affect the quality of your canned goods.

6. Pectin (if making jams and jellies)

Pectin is an optional ingredient for setting jams and jellies. It can help your preserves achieve the desired consistency.

7. Canning salt (if pickling)

When pickling, it's important to use canning salt, which is free of additives that could cloud the brine. Using table salt or iodized salt can lead to undesirable discoloration in your pickles.

8. Additional flavorings (optional)

Depending on your recipes, you may want to enhance the flavors with spices, herbs, or other flavorings. These can add a personal touch to your canned goods.

Now that you have all the necessary equipment and ingredients, you're ready to begin the water bath canning process. This method not only preserves the taste of different seasons but also captures the essence of each harvest, creating a time capsule of flavor and memory in every jar.

STEP-BY-STEP WATER BATH CANNING INSTRUCTIONS

Water bath canning is a delightful and rewarding process that allows you to capture the vibrant flavors of your favorite high-acid foods and preserve them for the year ahead.

By following these step-by-step instructions, you can ensure that each jar you create is a time capsule of taste and memory.

Step 1: Prepare Your Jars

1. Start by thoroughly washing your canning jars with hot, soapy water.
2. Inspect them for any chips or cracks.
3. To ensure your jars are clean and free from contaminants, sterilize them either in your water bath canner or your dishwasher.
4. Keep the jars warm until you're ready to use them.

Step 2: Prepare Your Recipe

1. Follow a trusted water bath canning recipe, ensuring you have the proper ingredients and measurements.
2. If you're making jams, jellies, or pickles, pay close attention to your recipe's instructions.

Step 3: Fill the Jars

1. Using a canning funnel, carefully fill your sterilized jars with the prepared food.
2. Be sure to leave the recommended headspace as specified in your recipe.
3. The headspace is the space between the food and the top of the jar, and it's crucial for achieving a proper seal.

Step 4: Remove Air Bubbles

1. Slide a bubble remover or non-metallic utensil along the inner edge of the jar to remove any trapped air bubbles. This step helps maintain the food's quality and safety.

Step 5: Wipe Jar Rims

1. Use a clean, damp cloth to wipe the rims of the jars, removing any residue.
2. A clean rim is essential for achieving a good seal.

Step 6: Apply Lids and Bands

1. Place a canning lid on each jar and then screw on the band until it is fingertip tight. This allows air to escape during processing while maintaining a proper seal.

Step 7: Process Jars

1. Place the filled jars in your water bath canner rack, ensuring they are covered by at least an inch of water.
2. Bring the water to a rolling boil.

Step 8: Set a Timer for Processing Time

1. Once the water is boiling, set a timer based on your recipe's processing time.
2. Accurate timing is crucial, as it varies depending on the food and jar size.

Step 9: Cool and Check Seals

1. After processing, remove the jars from the canner using a jar lifter and place them on a clean towel.
2. Allow the jars to cool at room temperature for 12 to 24 hours.
3. As they cool, you'll hear the satisfying "pop" sound as the lids seal.
4. Ensure that all jars are sealed properly by pressing the center of each lid. If it doesn't flex, the jar is sealed.

Step 10: Label and Store

1. Label each jar with the contents and the date of canning to help you identify what's inside.
2. Store your sealed jars in a cool, dark, and dry place.

By mastering these steps, you'll be able to capture the essence of each season, preserving the vibrant flavors of your favorite high-acid foods. Whether it's sweet jams, tangy pickles, or savory sauces, water bath canning is an art that ensures your pantry is stocked with homemade delights for the year ahead.

BEGINNER-FRIENDLY RECIPES FOR WATER BATH CANNING

Now, with the basic water bath instructions, you're ready to embark on your water bath canning journey. Here are some beginner-friendly recipes for you to try out.

Strawberry Jam

Ingredients:

- 4 cups fresh strawberries, hulled and chopped
- 4 cups granulated sugar
- ¼ cup of lemon juice

Directions:

1. Wash and hull the fresh strawberries, then chop them into small pieces.
2. In a large pot, combine the strawberries, sugar, and lemon juice. Allow the mixture to sit for about an hour to draw out the juice from the berries.
3. Bring the mixture to a boil, stirring frequently, and cook until the jam thickens (about 15–20 minutes).
4. While the jam is cooking, sterilize your canning jars and lids.
5. Once the jam is ready, ladle it into the sterilized jars, leaving about ¼-inch headspace.
6. Wipe the jar rims, apply the lids and bands, and tighten until fingertip tight.
7. Process the jars in a water bath canner for 10 minutes.
8. Remove the jars, allow them to cool, check the seals, label, and store.

Blueberry Preserves

Ingredients:

- 6 cups fresh blueberries
- 6 cups granulated sugar
- Zest from 2 lemons

Directions:

1. Wash the fresh blueberries and slightly crush them, leaving some whole for texture.
2. In a large pot, combine the blueberries, sugar, and lemon zest. Let it sit for an hour.
3. Bring the mixture to a boil and cook until it thickens (about 20–25 minutes).
4. Sterilize your canning jars and lids.
5. Fill the sterilized jars with the preserves, leaving about ¼-inch headspace.
6. Wipe the jar rims, apply lids and bands, and tighten until fingertip tight.
7. Process in a water bath canner for 10 minutes.
8. Remove the jars, cool, check seals, label, and store.

Bread and Butter Pickles

Ingredients:

- 5 cups sliced cucumbers
- 2 cups sliced onions
- ¼ cup pickling salt
- 2½ cups white sugar
- 2 cups distilled white vinegar
- 1 tbsp mustard seeds
- ½ tsp celery seeds
- ¼ tsp turmeric

Directions:

1. Slice cucumbers and onions and combine them in a large bowl with pickling salt. Let them sit for a few hours.
2. Rinse and drain the cucumbers and onions.
3. In a pot, combine sugar, vinegar, and spices. Bring to a boil.
4. Add the cucumber and onion mixture to the pot and cook for a few minutes.
5. Sterilize your canning jars and lids.
6. Fill jars with the pickle mixture, leaving about ½-inch headspace.
7. Wipe jar rims, apply lids and bands, and tighten until fingertip tight.
8. Process in a water bath canner for 10 minutes.
9. Remove jars, cool, check seals, label, and store.

Salsa

Ingredients:

- 10 cups chopped tomatoes
- 2 cups chopped onions
- 2 cups chopped bell peppers
- 2–4 chopped jalapeños (adjust to your preferred heat level)
- ½ cup chopped fresh cilantro
- 1½ cups white vinegar
- 1 tbsp salt

- 1 tsp ground cumin
- 1 tsp red pepper flakes (adjust to your preferred spiciness)

Directions:

1. Prepare tomatoes, onions, bell peppers, and jalapeños by chopping them finely.
2. In a pot, combine all the chopped ingredients with vinegar, salt, and spices.
3. Bring to a boil and simmer for 10–15 minutes.
4. Sterilize your canning jars and lids.
5. Fill jars with the salsa, leaving about ¼-inch headspace.
6. Wipe jar rims, apply lids and bands, and tighten until fingertip tight.
7. Process in a water bath canner for 15 minutes.
8. Remove jars, cool, check seals, label, and store.

Peach Chutney

Ingredients:

- 6 cups peeled, pitted, and chopped peaches
- 2 cups peeled, cored, and chopped apples
- 2 cups chopped onions
- 2½ cups brown sugar
- 2 cups vinegar
- ¼ cup of finely chopped ginger
- 1 tsp ground cinnamon
- ½ tsp ground cloves

Directions:

1. Peel, pit, and chop peaches, as well as peel, core, and chop apples. Dice onions.
2. In a pot, combine peaches, apples, onions, brown sugar, vinegar, ginger, and spices. Simmer until it thickens (about 30–40 minutes).
3. Sterilize your canning jars and lids.
4. Fill jars with the chutney, leaving about ¼-inch headspace.
5. Wipe jar rims, apply lids and bands, and tighten until fingertip tight.
6. Process in a water bath canner for 10 minutes.
7. Remove jars, cool, check seals, label, and store.

Raspberry Jam

Ingredients:

- 5 cups fresh raspberries
- 5 cups granulated sugar
- Juice of 2 lemons

Directions:

1. Rinse the fresh raspberries and crush them slightly.
2. In a large pot, combine the raspberries, sugar, and lemon juice. Allow the mixture to sit for about an hour to draw out the juice from the berries.

3. Bring the mixture to a boil, stirring frequently, and cook until the jam thickens (about 15–20 minutes).
4. While the jam is cooking, sterilize your canning jars and lids.
5. Once the jam is ready, ladle it into the sterilized jars, leaving about ¼-inch headspace.
6. Wipe the jar rims, apply the lids and bands, and tighten until fingertip tight.
7. Process the jars in a water bath canner for 10 minutes.
8. Remove the jars, allow them to cool, check the seals, label, and store.

Cherry Preserves

Ingredients:

- 4 cups fresh cherries, pitted and chopped
- 4 cups granulated sugar
- Zest from 1 orange
- Juice from 1 lemon

Directions:

1. Pit and chop the fresh cherries.
2. In a large pot, combine the cherries, sugar, orange zest, and lemon juice. Allow the mixture to sit for about an hour to draw out the juice from the cherries.
3. Bring the mixture to a boil, stirring frequently, and cook until the preserves thicken (about 20–25 minutes).

4. While the preserves are cooking, sterilize your canning jars and lids.
5. Once the preserves are ready, ladle them into the sterilized jars, leaving about ¼-inch headspace.
6. Wipe the jar rims, apply the lids and bands, and tighten until fingertip tight.
7. Process the jars in a water bath canner for 10 minutes.
8. Remove the jars, allow them to cool, check the seals, label, and store.

These recipes are designed with beginners in mind, making them accessible and easy to follow. They capture the essence of the seasons and allow you to create a colorful array of preserved delights for your pantry. Feel free to explore and enjoy the process of water bath canning!

In the next chapter, we'll explore the basics of pressure canning, take you through the process step by step, and provide you with beginner-friendly recipes to help you get started. Whether you're new to canning or have some experience, pressure canning will expand your food preservation skills and open up new culinary possibilities. Get ready for this exciting canning adventure!

7

UNDER PRESSURE

Someone once said, "Pressure makes diamonds." Now, we're not about to turn you into a jeweler, but we're here to tell you that pressure also makes safe and delicious preserved food. Welcome to the world of pressure canning, where you'll harness the power of pressure to create a treasure trove of preserved delights that go beyond high-acid foods. In this chapter, we'll delve into the mechanics of pressure canning and essential safety precautions and provide you with a selection of recipes crafted for this technique.

Pressure canning is a method of preserving food by using pressure to raise the temperature of the contents beyond the boiling point of water. It's a safe and effective way to can low-acid foods such as vegetables, meat, and poultry, eliminating harmful bacteria, yeasts, and molds.

Pressure canning achieves higher temperatures by trapping steam inside a sealed container, which increases the pressure.

As pressure rises, so does the temperature, enabling the safe preservation of low-acid foods.

Both pressure and temperature play crucial roles in killing harmful microorganisms. The combination of high pressure and elevated temperature ensures that bacteria, yeasts, and molds are effectively destroyed, making the food safe for long-term storage.

In pressure canning, temperatures can reach as high as 240–250° Fahrenheit (116–121° Celsius). These high temperatures are necessary to destroy the spores of Clostridium botulinum, a bacterium that can produce a deadly toxin in low-acid environments.

Pressure-canned food is extremely safe when processed correctly. By following proper procedures and maintaining the required pressure and processing times, you can ensure that your canned foods remain free of harmful microorganisms and toxins.

The processing time in pressure canning is determined by various factors, including the type of food, size of the jars, and altitude at which you are canning. It's crucial to consult reliable canning recipes or guides to determine the appropriate processing times for your situation.

To achieve safe pressure canning, it's essential to maintain a steady pressure throughout the process. This requires constant monitoring of the pressure gauge and making necessary adjustments to ensure that the pressure remains within the recommended range.

Pressure canning is a valuable skill for preserving a wide range of foods, allowing you to enjoy your favorite dishes year-round. It's important to follow trusted recipes and guidelines to ensure the safety and quality of your home-canned products.

PERFECT FOR PRESSURE: IDEAL FOODS FOR PRESSURE CANNING

Pressure canning is an excellent method for preserving low-acid foods, as it provides the necessary conditions to ensure their safety and long-term storage.

Always follow tested and approved recipes and guidelines for pressure canning to ensure the safety and quality of your preserved foods.

Here are some examples of low-acid foods that are well-suited for pressure canning:

1. Green beans

Benefits of pressure canning: Green beans retain their crispness and vibrant green color when pressure canned. This method allows you to enjoy the freshness of garden-picked green beans throughout the year.

Versatility: Properly canned green beans maintain their texture and taste, making them versatile ingredients for various dishes, from casseroles to stir-fries.

2. Carrots

Preserving natural sweetness: Pressure canning preserves the natural sweetness and firm texture of carrots. Canned carrots are excellent for use in soups, stews, or as a delightful side dish.

Convenience: Canned carrots maintain their flavor and nutritional value, providing a convenient addition to your pantry for quick and easy meal preparation.

3. Corn

Retaining sweet flavor: Corn is another low-acid vegetable that responds well to pressure canning. Canned corn retains its sweet flavor and crispness, making it a versatile ingredient for various recipes, from succotash to corn chowder.

Year-round availability: Pressure canning allows you to enjoy the taste of fresh corn throughout the year, even when it's out of season.

4. Peas

Tenderness and sweetness: Pressure-canned peas are tender and delicious, perfect for adding to side dishes or incorporating into casseroles.

Vibrant appearance: Canned peas maintain their vibrant color and natural sweetness, making them a welcome addition to your canned goods collection.

5. Meats (beef, pork, poultry, and game meats)

Tenderness: Pressure canning is a safe and effective method for preserving various types of meat. Canned meat is tender and can be used in a wide range of dishes, such as soups, stews, and casseroles.

Protein source: Canned meat provides a convenient source of protein for your pantry, and when canned correctly, it retains its flavor and nutritional value.

6. Seafood (salmon, tuna, and shrimp)

Quick and convenient protein: Low-acid seafood can be effectively preserved through pressure canning, providing a quick and convenient source of protein.

Versatility: Canned seafood is a versatile ingredient for various recipes, from pasta dishes to salads and chowders.

7. Beans and legumes (black beans, kidney beans, lentils)

Extended shelf life: Dried beans and legumes can be pressure canned to extend their shelf life. This is especially handy if you enjoy making dishes like chili, bean soups, or salads regularly.

Maintaining natural flavors: Pressure canning ensures that beans and legumes are readily available for your culinary creations and maintain their natural flavors and textures.

8. Soups and stews (homemade soups and stews)

Time-saving strategy: Pressure-canning homemade soups and stews containing low-acid ingredients like vegetables and meat is a time-saving strategy.

Year-round enjoyment: Canned soups and stews retain their flavors and nutritional value, allowing you to enjoy your favorite homemade meals year-round.

9. Stocks and broths (chicken, beef, or vegetable stocks)

Flavorful base: Homemade stocks and broths are excellent for pressure canning. They serve as a flavorful base for many recipes and add depth to your dishes.

Convenience: Pressure canning preserves the rich flavors of these stocks, allowing you to enhance the taste of your dishes without the need for time-consuming preparation.

10. Sauces (spaghetti sauce and salsa)

Preserving homemade condiments: If you make your own low-acid pasta sauces or salsas, pressure canning is an excellent way to preserve them for future use.

Convenience: Canned pasta sauces and salsas lock in the flavors and allow you to enjoy your homemade condiments year-round, serving as a convenient addition to your pantry.

11. Chili (classic beef or vegetarian chili)

Ready to use: Pressure canning is an ideal method for storing your favorite chili recipes. Canned chili is ready to use whenever you need it, whether you prefer a classic beef chili or a vegetarian version.

Retaining favors: Canned chili retains its flavors, making it a convenient and time-saving addition to your pantry for quick and satisfying meals.

When pressure canning low-acid foods, it's crucial to follow approved canning recipes and guidelines to ensure proper processing times and safety. This ensures that you create a variety of delicious and safe preserved foods that you can enjoy throughout the year while maintaining the quality and taste of your ingredients.

PRESSURE CANNING WITH CARE: A DETAILED WALKTHROUGH

Pressure canning is a fantastic method for preserving low-acid foods safely. By following this step-by-step guide, you'll be well-prepared to start your pressure canning journey. Before we dive into a detailed walkthrough of the pressure canning process—to ensure that you're well-prepared for your journey—let's first take a look at the equipment you'll need.

Pressure Canner

To begin, you need a reliable pressure canner. It should have a tight-sealing lid, an accurate pressure gauge, and a safety valve.

1. Tight-sealing lid

   - seals the pressure canner tight during canning to keep the steam in check
   - usually made of aluminum or stainless steel

2. Pressure gauge

   - keeps tabs on the pressure inside for a safe canning experience
   - dial gauges have a face with pressure markings; weighted gauges—which we'll talk about in a moment—have a pressure regulator

3. Safety valve

   - lets out extra pressure to avoid any canner explosions
   - usually made of sturdy metal or something that can handle the heat

4. Vent pipe

   - this lets out the steam as needed
   - made to handle some serious heat

5. Pressure regulator

- controls and maintains the pressure inside the canner
- weighted for weighted gauge canners; adjustable for dial gauge canners

There are two main types of pressure canners: dial gauge and weighted gauge. Both types are effective, but it's crucial to follow the manufacturer's instructions specific to your canner model.

Dial gauge pressure canner: The daily gauge has a nifty dial on the lid to show you the pressure inside. You'll need to keep an eye on it and give it an accuracy check once a year.

Weighted gauge pressure canner: This one has a weight on the vent pipe that rocks or jiggles to tell you the pressure. These canners don't need a yearly check-in and are straightforward to use and reliable.

When choosing the right pressure canner there are a few tips you can keep in mind:

1. Size matters

- Choose based on how much food you're planning to can.
- Most canners fit quart-sized jars.

2. Material

- Pressure canners come in aluminum or stainless steel.
- Stainless steel is durable but can be a little on the heavy side.

3. Brands and models

- Look into trusted brands like Presto, All American, or Mirro.
- Seriously, follow the manufacturer's playbook.

4. Can it take care of business?

- Make sure all parts are in tip-top shape.
- Remember that dial gauges may need a yearly test.

Jars and Lids

Make sure you use canning jars that are in good condition and free of cracks or chips. The quart jar is the most common size, but you can choose different sizes based on your needs. Additionally, ensure you have new, properly fitting canning lids and bands. The quality of your jars and lids is essential for achieving a proper seal.

Let's take a peek at some of the most popular jars used in pressure canning:

1. Mason jars

- the most common choice
- sturdy and widely available
- come in various sizes, with regular or wide mouths

2. Ball jars

- a popular brand of mason jars
- trusted quality
- available in diverse sizes and styles

3. Kerr jars

- another reputable brand of mason jars
- well-regarded for canning purposes
- similar to Ball jars in size and options

4. Weck jars

- distinctive with a rubber gasket and glass lid
- European design; gaining popularity
- a bit pricier but offers a unique aesthetic

5. Bernardin jars

- popular in Canada

- well-regarded for canning
- similar to mason jars

6. Quattro Stagioni jars

- Italian brand
- high-quality glass
- unique design; suitable for canning

When buying jars to use for pressure canning, there are a couple of important considerations that you need to keep in mind:

1. Size matters

- Choose jar sizes based on your canning needs.
- Common sizes include quart, pint, and half-pint.

2. Material

- Opt for tempered glass jars designed for canning.
- Ensure they can withstand the high temperatures of pressure canning.

3. Mouth type

- Decide between regular and wide-mouth jars.
- Wide mouths are convenient for packing and unpacking.

4. Check for canning approval

- Look for jars explicitly labeled as suitable for canning.
- Confirm that they meet safety standards.

5. Reusable lids

- Consider using two-piece metal lids for a secure seal.
- Check for any signs of wear and tear after each use.

Always follow the manufacturer's guidelines for the specific jar you choose. This ensures you're using them correctly and safely for pressure canning.

Low-Acid Foods

Prepare the low-acid foods you intend to can—like the ones we discussed in the previous section, including vegetables, meats, or other suitable ingredients. Ensure you wash and prepare the food according to the recipe's instructions. High-quality ingredients are crucial for a successful canning process.

When preparing low-acid foods for pressure canning, follow these essential steps to ensure a successful and safe canning process:

1. Selecting ingredients

- Choose fresh, high-quality ingredients for the best results.

- Use vegetables like green beans, carrots, and corn, or meats such as beef, poultry, or seafood.

2. Washing and cleaning

- Thoroughly wash all fruits, vegetables, and meats under cool, running water.
- Remove any dirt, debris, or foreign materials.
- Trim and discard any bruised or damaged portions.

3. Peeling and trimming

- For certain vegetables and fruits, such as carrots or peaches, peel or trim as required.
- Remove skins, bones, and excess fat from meats.

4. Cutting and slicing

- Cut vegetables and fruits into uniform pieces to ensure even cooking.
- Cut meats into chunks or cubes, considering the size of your canning jars.

5. Following recipe instructions

- Adhere to the canning recipe's instructions regarding ingredient preparation.
- Some recipes may require blanching, parboiling, or pre-cooking certain ingredients.

6. Avoiding contamination

- Practice good hygiene to prevent contamination.
- Wash hands thoroughly before handling ingredients.
- Use clean and sanitized utensils, cutting boards, and surfaces.

7. Maintaining quality

- Handle ingredients gently to preserve their texture and flavor.
- Minimize exposure to air to prevent oxidation.

8. Measuring ingredients

- Accurately measure ingredients according to the canning recipe.
- Follow recommended ratios to ensure a safe canning process.

9. Controlling temperature

- Keep perishable ingredients refrigerated until you are ready to process them.
- Work efficiently to maintain the freshness and quality of the ingredients.

Remember to choose canning recipes from reputable sources, such as the United States Department of Agriculture (USDA) or trusted canning guides, and always follow recipes that provide precise instructions for low-acid foods.

Clean Work Area

Before starting the pressure canning process, ensure that your work area, equipment, and jars are clean and sanitized. This is a critical step to prevent contamination of your preserved foods. Use hot, soapy water to clean your equipment, and consider sterilizing your jars in boiling water or using a dishwasher with a sterilized setting.

1. Clear and organize

   - Begin by clearing your work area of any unnecessary items.
   - Organize your canning equipment and ingredients for easy access.

2. Wash hands thoroughly

   - Wash your hands with soap and warm water before handling any canning equipment or ingredients.

3. Clean surfaces

   - Wipe down all surfaces, including countertops and tables, with a clean, damp cloth.
   - Ensure there are no residues or debris that could contaminate your work area.

4. Sanitize equipment

- Use hot, soapy water to thoroughly clean all canning equipment, including jars, lids, bands, and tools.
- Pay special attention to areas that come into direct contact with food.

5. Sterilize jars

- Consider sterilizing your canning jars to eliminate any potential bacteria.
- Submerge the jars in boiling water for 10 minutes or use the sterilize setting on a dishwasher.

6. Inspect jars

- Check each jar for cracks, chips, or defects.
- Discard any jars that show signs of damage, as they may compromise the canning process.

7. Prepare a sterile workspace

- Lay out clean, sanitized towels or paper towels to place hot jars on during the canning process.
- Avoid using towels with strong fragrances that could transfer to your preserved foods.

8. Clean canning area

- If you have a dedicated canning area, clean and sanitize it regularly to maintain a hygienic environment.
- Check shelves and storage areas for dust or debris.

9. Avoid cross-contamination

- Use separate cutting boards for meats and vegetables to prevent cross-contamination.
- Clean cutting boards, knives, and utensils between different types of ingredients.

10. Maintain personal hygiene

- Tie back long hair and avoid touching your face or hair during the canning process.
- Consider wearing a clean apron to minimize the risk of contaminating the work area.

By following these steps, you'll create a clean and organized workspace for your pressure canning activities, reducing the risk of contamination and ensuring the safety of your preserved foods.

Now that you have all your equipment and ingredients ready, you can proceed with the pressure canning process. This detailed guide will walk you through the essential steps, allowing you to confidently and safely preserve low-acid foods.

HOW TO PRESERVE FOOD USING THE PRESSURE CANNING METHOD

Preserving food using the pressure canning method is a fantastic way to ensure the safety and longevity of low-acid foods.

Here's a detailed guide to help you master the pressure canning process:

Step 1: Understand the Pressure Canner

1. Before pressurizing, let the canner release steam to remove air.
2. Keep the heat at the right level for the recommended pressure.
3. Allow the canner to cool before opening it.
4. Always follow the manufacturer's instructions.
5. Stick to approved canning recipes for safety.
6. Wait for the canner to cool before opening.
7. Regularly check your canner for wear, rust, or anything unusual.

Step 2: Prepare Jars and Lids

1. Wash jars, lids, and bands with hot, soapy water.
2. Rinse well to remove any dirt.
3. Keep jars warm to prevent them from breaking when filled.

Step 3: Fill the Jars

1. Use a funnel to easily fill jars with your prepared food.
2. Leave space at the top as guided by your recipe.

Step 4: Remove Air Bubbles and Wipe Jar Rims

1. Use a tool or spatula to remove air bubbles by running it along the inside.
2. Wipe the rims of the jars with a clean, damp cloth to remove any residue.

Step 5: Apply Lids and Bands and Prepare the Canner

1. Place lids on jars and secure them with bands.
2. Don't overtighten; leave some room for air to escape.
3. Follow your canner's instructions for how much water to add.

Step 6: Seal and Pressurize

1. Make sure the canner's lid is tightly closed.
2. Allow steam to vent for 10 minutes to remove air.
3. Close the vent and reach the recommended pressure as per your recipe.

Step 7: Process

1. Keep the pressure steady according to your recipe's instructions.

2. Turn off the heat and let the canner cool down naturally.
3. Carefully open the canner and use a lifter to remove the jars.

Step 8: Test Seals, Label, and Store

1. After cooling, check the lids for proper seals.
2. Press the center; it should be concave, indicating a good seal.
3. Label each jar with its contents and the date of canning.
4. Store the sealed jars in a cool, dark, dry place.
5. Consume within a year for the best quality.

By following these steps, beginners can confidently and safely preserve low-acid foods using the pressure canning method. Stick to the instructions, use approved recipes, and enjoy the benefits of home-canned foods.

BEGINNER-FRIENDLY RECIPES FOR PRESSURE CANNING

These recipes offer a diverse range of flavors and ingredients for your pressure canning endeavors. Remember to follow proper canning procedures and guidelines to ensure the safety and quality of your preserved foods. Enjoy your culinary creations!

Pressure-Canned Salsa

This is a vibrant salsa bursting with the flavors of fresh tomatoes, onions, bell peppers, cilantro, and garlic. Enhanced with a hint of cumin and balanced with vinegar, this zesty salsa is pressure-canned to preserve its freshness. It's perfect for dipping, topping, or adding a kick to any dish.

Ingredients:

- 15 lbs tomatoes, peeled and diced
- 3 cups onions, finely chopped
- 2 cups bell peppers, finely chopped
- ½ cup fresh cilantro, chopped
- 4 cloves garlic, minced
- 1 cup vinegar (5% acidity)
- 2 tsp salt
- ½ tsp cumin (optional)

Directions:

1. Combine all the ingredients in a large pot and bring to a boil.
2. Reduce heat and simmer for 10 minutes, stirring occasionally.
3. Ladle the hot salsa into sterilized quart jars, leaving ½-inch headspace.
4. Wipe the jar rims, place lids, and bands, and tighten just until fingertip tight.

5. Process in a pressure canner at 10 pounds pressure (adjust for altitude) for 15 minutes.
6. Allow jars to cool, check for proper seals, label, and store.

Classic Beef Stew

Hearty chunks of beef, paired with carrots, potatoes, onions, and celery, create a classic beef stew. Simmered in a rich broth with tomato paste, salt, and pepper, this comforting stew is pressure-canned to perfection. Enjoy the convenience of a delicious, ready-to-heat meal anytime.

Ingredients:

- 4 lbs beef chunks
- 3 cups carrots, sliced
- 3 cups potatoes, diced
- 2 cups onions, chopped
- 1 cup celery, chopped
- 8 cups beef broth
- ¼ cup tomato paste
- 2 tsp salt
- ½ tsp black pepper

Directions:

- Brown the beef chunks in a large pot.
- Add the vegetables and sauté for a few minutes.
- Stir in the beef broth, tomato paste, salt, and pepper.

- Simmer until the beef is tender and the stew is flavorful.
- Pack the hot stew into sterilized quart jars, leaving 1-inch headspace.
- Wipe the jar rims, place lids, and bands, and tighten just until fingertip tight.
- Process in a pressure canner at 10 pounds pressure (adjust for altitude) for 90 minutes.
- Allow jars to cool, check for proper seals, label, and store.

Spicy Black Bean Soup

This is a soul-warming soup featuring tender black beans, onions, garlic, tomatoes, and a blend of spices. With a touch of lime for brightness, this spicy black bean soup is pressure-canned to lock in its robust flavors. It's a versatile and convenient option for quick, flavorful meals.

Ingredients:

- 3 cups dried black beans, soaked and drained
- 2 cups onions, chopped
- 4 cloves garlic, minced
- 4 cups tomatoes, diced
- 6 cups vegetable broth
- 2 tsp ground cumin
- 1 tsp chili powder
- 1 tsp salt
- Juice of 2 limes

Directions:

1. Combine all ingredients in a large pot and bring to a boil.
2. Reduce heat and simmer until the beans are tender and the flavors meld.
3. Pack the hot soup into sterilized quart jars, leaving 1-inch headspace.
4. Wipe the jar rims, place lids, and bands, and tighten just until fingertip tight.
5. Process in a pressure canner at 10 pounds pressure (adjust for altitude) for 75 minutes.
6. Allow jars to cool, check for proper seals, label, and store.

Chicken Curry

Indulge in the aromatic and savory flavors of chicken curry with coconut milk, curry paste, bell peppers, onions, garlic, and ginger. Pressure-canned to perfection, this chicken curry is a time-saving delight. Enjoy a taste of homemade curry whenever you desire.

Ingredients:

- 4 lbs chicken chunks
- 4 cups coconut milk
- ½ cup curry paste
- 2 cups bell peppers, sliced
- 2 cups onions, chopped

- 4 cloves garlic, minced
- 2 in. piece ginger, minced
- 2 tsp salt
- ½ cup fresh cilantro, chopped

Directions:

1. Prepare the curry by sautéing the onions, garlic, and ginger.
2. Add the chicken, coconut milk, curry paste, bell peppers, and salt.
3. Simmer until the chicken is fully cooked and tender.
4. Pack the hot chicken curry into sterilized quart jars, ensuring chicken pieces are submerged, and leave 1-inch headspace.
5. Wipe the jar rims, place lids, and bands, and tighten just until fingertip tight.
6. Process in a pressure canner at 10 pounds pressure (adjust for altitude) for 75 minutes.
7. Allow jars to cool, check for proper seals, label, and store.

Canned Corned Beef

Tender chunks of corned beef, infused with pickling spices, garlic, and bay leaves, create a savory canned corned beef. Cooked to perfection and preserved in its flavorful juices, this recipe is ideal for adding a delicious twist to sandwiches, salads, or casseroles.

Ingredients:

- 4 lbs corned beef brisket
- 4 cups water
- 2 tbsp pickling spices
- 4 cloves garlic
- 2 bay leaves

Directions:

1. Cook the corned beef brisket according to package instructions, then allow it to cool.
2. Slice the cooked beef into 1-inch chunks.
3. Pack the chunks into sterilized quart jars, adding a clove of garlic, ½ tbsp pickling spices, and ½ bay leaf to each jar.
4. Ladle the cooking liquid over the beef, leaving 1-inch headspace.
5. Wipe the jar rims, place lids, and bands, and tighten just until fingertip tight.
6. Process in a pressure canner at 10 pounds pressure (adjust for altitude) for 75 minutes.
7. Allow jars to cool, check for proper seals, label, and store.

Italian Pasta Sauce

A luscious blend of tomatoes, onions, garlic, fresh basil, and aromatic herbs creates an Italian pasta sauce. Slow-cooked to perfection and pressure-canned, this versatile sauce adds an authentic Italian touch to your favorite pasta dishes.

Ingredients:

- 12 lbs tomatoes, peeled and diced
- 2 cups onions, chopped
- ¼ cup garlic, minced
- ¼ cup fresh basil, chopped
- 2 tbsp dried oregano
- 1 tbsp dried thyme
- ¼ cup olive oil
- 2 tbsp salt
- ¼ cup sugar

Directions:

1. Cook the sauce until it thickens and flavors meld.
2. Ladle the hot sauce into sterilized quart jars, leaving ½-inch headspace.
3. Wipe the jar rims, place lids, and bands, and tighten just until fingertip tight.
4. Process in a pressure canner at 10 pounds pressure (adjust for altitude) for 35 minutes.
5. Allow jars to cool, check for proper seals, label, and store.

Mixed Vegetable Medley

Experience the vibrant colors and flavors of a mixed vegetable medley featuring carrots, green beans, corn, peas, bell peppers, onions, and garlic. Blanching preserves the crispness, and pressure canning ensures a ready-to-use assortment for various recipes.

Ingredients:

- 4 cups carrots, sliced
- 4 cups green beans, cut into 1 in. pieces
- 4 cups corn kernels
- 4 cups peas
- 2 cups bell peppers, diced
- 2 cups onions, chopped
- 4 cloves garlic, minced
- 6 cups vegetable broth
- 2 tsp salt
- ½ tsp black pepper

Directions:

1. Blanch the vegetables in boiling water for a few minutes, then immediately transfer to an ice bath.
2. Pack the blanched vegetables into sterilized quart jars, leaving 1-inch headspace.
3. Pour hot vegetable broth over the vegetables.
4. Wipe the jar rims, place lids, and bands, and tighten just until fingertip tight.

5. Process in a pressure canner at 10 pounds pressure (adjust for altitude) for 60 minutes.
6. Allow jars to cool, check for proper seals, label, and store.

Pork and Beans

Savor the classic combination of navy beans and pork, elevated with a sweet and tangy molasses, brown sugar, mustard, and spice blend. Pressure-canned for convenience, these pork and beans are a delightful addition to your pantry.

Ingredients:

- 4 cups navy beans, soaked and drained
- 4 cups pork chunks
- 1 cup molasses
- ½ cup brown sugar
- 2 tbsp mustard
- 2 tsp salt
- ½ tsp black pepper

Directions:

1. Cook the beans and pork until they are tender.
2. Pack the beans and pork into sterilized quart jars, leaving 1-inch headspace.
3. Combine molasses, brown sugar, mustard, salt, and pepper in a saucepan, and heat until well combined.
4. Pour the hot sauce over the beans and pork in each jar.

5. Wipe the jar rims, place lids, and bands, and tighten just until fingertip tight.

6. Process in a pressure canner at 10 pounds pressure (adjust for altitude) for 75 minutes.

7. Allow jars to cool, check for proper seals, label, and store.

Chunky Chicken Soup

This is a comforting and chunky chicken soup loaded with chicken, carrots, potatoes, celery, onions, and garlic. Simmered in a flavorful chicken broth with thyme, salt, and pepper, this hearty soup is pressure-canned for a quick and wholesome meal.

Ingredients:

- 4 lbs chicken chunks
- 3 cups carrots, sliced
- 3 cups potatoes, diced
- 2 cups celery, sliced
- 2 cups onions, chopped
- 4 cloves garlic, minced
- 8 cups chicken broth
- 1 tsp dried thyme
- 2 tsp salt
- ½ tsp black pepper

Directions:

1. Combine all ingredients in a large pot and simmer until the chicken and vegetables are tender.
2. Pack the hot soup into sterilized quart jars, leaving 1-inch headspace.
3. Wipe the jar rims, place lids, and bands, and tighten just until fingertip tight.
4. Process in a pressure canner at 10 pounds pressure (adjust for altitude) for 75 minutes.
5. Allow jars to cool, check for proper seals, label, and store.

These instructions should help you successfully prepare and can a variety of delicious low-acid foods. Always prioritize safety and adhere to approved canning recipes and guidelines for the best results. Enjoy your culinary creations!

The next chapter, "Canning Conundrums," will address common challenges and issues that can arise during the canning process, providing solutions and insights to help you navigate these conundrums successfully and ensure your canning experiences remain enjoyable and your preserved foods safe and delicious.

8

CANNING CONUNDRUMS

Let me take you back to my first attempt at canning: There I was, armed with a bunch of garden goodies, excited to fill my pantry with homemade treats. I was ready for a triumphant canning adventure, filled with hopes of delicious meals—but reality hit me hard.

As I cracked open my jars, expecting a feast, disappointment washed over me. The jars I spent hours preparing didn't seal properly. My dreamy jam, meant for warm toast, turned out disappointingly runny. Some jars had floating fruit, and my once-clear preserves looked cloudy. It was a canning puzzle, and I was determined to solve it.

Instead of letting this setback get me down, I turned it into an opportunity to learn. I wanted to understand where I went wrong, gain knowledge, and get better at canning. Over time, I realized that canning isn't just about being creative; it's a skill that you can master with a bit of science.

This chapter is like a diary of the lessons I picked up during my canning adventures. I'm excited to share these insights, not just as a story about my experiences but as a guide for anyone facing similar canning challenges.

In these pages, we dive into the common problems you might face during canning. Whether you're a newbie trying canning for the first time or a pro looking to polish your skills, these issues are something we all deal with. But fear not! With the right know-how and techniques, these challenges aren't road-blocks. They're more like stepping stones that lead to canned goodies you can be proud of.

Now, let's journey on and tackle canning conundrums, break down the complexities, and equip you with the tips and tricks to turn your canning adventures into a source of kitchen pride.

CANNING JARS DIDN'T SEAL: TROUBLESHOOTING AND SOLUTIONS

Discovering that your carefully canned jars didn't seal properly can be a real downer. I've been there, feeling that mix of disappointment and frustration. Let's unravel the mystery behind unsealed jars and explore how to make sure those lids stay securely in place.

1. Inadequate cleaning or sterilization

Issue: If jar rims aren't thoroughly cleaned or sterilized, contaminants may hinder the sealing process.
Solution: Before filling jars, ensure they are impeccably

clean. Use hot, soapy water for washing and sterilize by boiling or using a dishwasher with a sterilized setting.

2. Incorrect headspace

Issue: Failing to maintain the recommended headspace can lead to air entrapment and prevent a proper seal.
Solution: Follow the recipe's specific guidelines for headspace. Headspace allows for expansion during processing, ensuring an effective seal.

3. Deformed or damaged lids

Issue: Lids that are bent, dented, or damaged won't create a secure seal.
Solution: Inspect lids before use and choose new, undamaged lids and bands. Also, discard any lids with visible defects to ensure a proper seal.

Unsealed jars are a common challenge in home canning, but with thorough preparation and swift action, you can minimize these setbacks and enjoy successfully preserved foods.

1. Thoroughly clean and sterilize

- Wash jars with hot water and soap, emphasizing thorough cleaning of jar rims.
- Residue on the rim can disrupt the sealing process, so ensure it's free of any debris.

- Boil jars for 10 minutes or utilize a dishwasher's sterilized setting.
- Sterilized jars provide an ideal environment for creating a secure seal during the canning process.

2. Ensure appropriate headspace

- Each canning recipe specifies the required headspace, which is crucial for proper sealing.
- Adhering to these guidelines ensures there's adequate room for expansion during processing and prevents issues like siphoning.

3. Use new, undamaged lids and bands

- Before canning, carefully inspect each lid for any deformities, dents, or damages.
- Damaged lids can compromise the integrity of the seal and should be discarded.
- Opt for new lids and bands for each canning session to ensure optimal sealing.
- Reusing lids increases the risk of seal failure, so it's advisable to use fresh ones each time.

Sometimes, you can inspect all the lids and jars and follow all the right steps but still have a problem jar that does not want to seal.

What do you do when the jar just doesn't want to seal?

1. Reprocess promptly

Check each jar for a proper seal after processing. An unsealed jar will have a lid that has not been sucked down. Promptly reprocess unsealed jars according to the recipe's instructions to achieve a secure seal.

2. Refrigerate and consume

If reprocessing isn't feasible, promptly refrigerate the unsealed jars to prevent spoilage. Plan to use the contents within a few days to maintain quality and safety.

Ensuring your jars are sealed properly is essential for safe and successful home canning. By following these steps, you'll minimize the risk of unsealed jars and enjoy the satisfaction of well-preserved foods.

JAM OR JELLIES ARE RUNNY

Discovering that your meticulously prepared jam has a runny consistency can be disheartening. However, understanding the reasons behind it and knowing how to rectify the issue can turn the situation around.

Cooking jam is a delicate dance of time and temperature. If the jam doesn't undergo the necessary cooking duration, it might not reach the optimum setting point. Pectin is a natural thickening agent found in fruits, and it needs sufficient heat and time to activate and create the gel-like structure characteristic of jams and jellies.

Ensure that you adhere to the recommended cooking times in your recipe. Use a reliable candy or jam thermometer to monitor the temperature accurately. This guarantees that the pectin is activated, leading to a properly set jam.

1. Not enough pectin

Pectin is a crucial component for achieving the desired consistency in jams and jellies. If there's a shortage of pectin, the mixture might remain too liquid.

Solution: Be attentive to the natural pectin levels in your chosen fruits. Some fruits are naturally low in pectin, and commercial pectin can be introduced to compensate. Follow the recommended pectin quantities in your recipe or adjust accordingly if using a different type of pectin.

2. Incorrect ratio of sugar to fruit

The ratio of sugar to fruit is not just a matter of taste; it plays a fundamental role in the setting of jams and jellies. Sugar acts as a preservative and contributes to the gel formation. Deviations from the recommended ratio can result in an upset, runny product.

Solution: Always measure your ingredients precisely, especially when it comes to sugar and fruit. Don't be tempted to reduce sugar content significantly, as it directly influences the preservation and texture of your final product. Follow the recipe diligently to strike the right balance.

The relationship between cooking time, pectin content, sugar ratio, and fruit type is intricate. Mastering this interplay is key to consistently achieving the perfect set in your jams and jellies. Paying attention to these details will empower you to troubleshoot and refine your canning skills, ensuring delicious, well-set preserves every time.

To ensure perfect consistency, here are a couple of preventive measures you can keep in mind:

1. Always follow the recipe's cooking and pectin recommendations

Cooking times in jam and jelly recipes are not arbitrary; they are carefully calculated to activate pectin and set the mixture. Deviating from these times can lead to inconsistency.

Actionable step: Invest in a reliable candy or jam thermometer to monitor the cooking temperature accurately. Trust the recommended times in your recipe to achieve the perfect balance of flavor and texture.

2. Pectin precision

Remember pectin is the magic ingredient that transforms fruit blends into delightful spreads. Using the right amount, as suggested by the recipe, ensures that the pectin activates appropriately for the desired consistency.

Actionable step: Familiarize yourself with the natural pectin levels in different fruits. Adjust pectin quantities if necessary, following your recipe or the guidelines provided with commercial pectin.

3. Measure ingredients accurately

The delicate balance between sugar and fruit is the essence of well-set jams and jellies. Accurate measurements are crucial for achieving the perfect interplay.

Actionable step: Use precise measuring tools, especially for ingredients like sugar and fruit. Eyeballing can lead to imbalances, affecting the overall texture and taste. Follow the recipe meticulously to maintain consistency.

By meticulously adhering to recommended cooking times, pectin quantities, and precise measurements, you set the stage for consistently achieving the perfect texture in your jams and jellies. Let the science behind the recipes guide you, and your future batches will be a testament to the art of well-preserved goodness.

Should you run into a sticky—or in this runny—situation, you can recook the jam or jelly with additional pectin or sugar.

1. Return your runny jam to the stove, giving it another chance at perfection.
2. Add more pectin based on the product's instructions to bolster its setting power.
3. Bring the mixture to a gentle boil, ensuring a consistent stir to incorporate the added pectin.

4. Continue stirring until your jam thickens to the desired, luscious consistency.

You can follow the next steps when adding extra sugar.

1. Gradually introduce more sugar into the runny jam, providing a sweet solution to the consistency issue.
2. Stir persistently until the sugar dissolves completely, contributing to the jam's overall thickness.
3. Continue the cooking process until your jam achieves the delightful thickness you desire.

Regularly inspect the evolving texture of your jam or jelly during the recooking process. Adjust the amount of added pectin or sugar based on your observations, ensuring a harmonious blend.

By understanding the causes of runny jams or jellies and taking proactive measures, you empower yourself to enhance your future canning endeavors. Moreover, the ability to rescue a runny batch showcases the resilience and adaptability of home canning, turning a potential disappointment into a triumph of preservation prowess.

DEALING WITH LIQUID SPILLAGE WHEN CANNING: UNPACKING CAUSES AND EFFECTIVE SOLUTIONS

Encountering unexpected spills while canning can be disheartening, but understanding the reasons behind them and knowing how to address the issues is crucial. Let's explore the common causes of liquid spills during the canning process and practical steps to prevent and manage them.

1. Overfilling the jars

Explanation: Filling jars beyond the recommended headspace can result in excess pressure during processing, causing liquids to overflow.

Solution: Adhere strictly to the specified headspace guidelines provided in your canning recipe, allowing room for necessary expansion.

2. Sudden temperature changes

Explanation: Rapid shifts in temperature, such as placing hot jars on a cold surface, can lead to internal pressure changes and liquid leakage.

Solution: Ensure a gradual cooling process by placing hot jars on a towel or wooden surface, avoiding direct contact with colder surfaces.

3. Poorly tightened bands

Explanation: Bands that are not adequately tightened may allow liquid seepage during processing.

Solution: Tighten lids securely following recommended guidelines—firm enough to form a seal but not excessively tight.

To prevent these spilling mishaps, you can make use of the following preventive measures:

1. Follow recommended headspace guidelines

Adequate headspace is essential for accommodating necessary expansion and contraction during processing. Refer to your canning recipe for specific headspace recommendations and follow them meticulously.

2. Allow jars to cool gradually

Gradual cooling minimizes pressure changes within the jars, reducing the risk of liquid spills. Place hot jars on a towel or wooden surface, steering clear of direct contact with colder surfaces.

3. Ensure lids are tightened appropriately

Properly tightened lids are critical for maintaining the integrity of the seal. Tighten lids according to recommended guidelines —fingertight, allowing for some flexibility while ensuring security.

Should any spills occur, you need to take the appropriate action. Carefully clean the exterior of jars to remove any residue from spilled liquid. A clean jar exterior is essential for achieving a proper seal during reprocessing. Then, replace lids and reprocess only if necessary. If spillage is significant or if the seal is compromised, replace the lids and reprocess the jars. This step ensures the safety and quality of your canned goods.

Understanding the dynamics behind liquid spills during processing empowers you to take proactive measures. By incorporating these preventive strategies and promptly addressing spills when they occur, you can enhance the success and safety of your home canning endeavors.

UNDERSTANDING AND ADDRESSING FOOD DARKENING IN CANNING: PRESERVING VISUAL APPEAL

Discovering a dark layer at the top of your jar can be disconcerting, but fear not—we'll unravel the reasons behind this phenomenon and equip you with practical methods to maintain the visual allure of your home-canned goods.

There are two common causes why the food at the top starts to darken, namely oxidation and inadequate headspace.

1. Oxidation

When food is exposed to air during the canning process, oxidation can occur, resulting in darkening at the top. It's like the browning of an apple slice left out; a similar process can affect canned goods.

2. Inadequate headspace

If there's not enough headspace in the jar, the food can press against the lid, promoting discoloration. Imagine the pressure causing a portion of the food to touch the lid, leading to changes in color.

Although these are the two most common causes why the top layer of food will darken, there are other reasons as well.

1. Temperature variations during processing

Uneven temperatures during the canning process can lead to variations in color. Certain parts of the food are being exposed to slightly higher temperatures, causing localized darkening.

2. Mineral content in water

The mineral content in the water used for canning might interact with the food, causing changes in color. Similar to how minerals in water can affect the color of boiled vegetables, this interaction can impact canned goods.

3. Natural variability in ingredients

Some fruits and vegetables naturally have variations in color due to factors like ripeness and growing conditions. Just as the color of apples can vary, even within the same batch, the top of the jar may showcase this natural variability.

4. Reaction with jar materials

Interaction between the food and the materials of the canning jar, especially if it contains metals, can contribute to discoloration. A slight chemical reaction between the food and the jar influences the color.

5. Prolonged storage

Over an extended storage period, even if the jar is sealed, some changes in color might occur. Similar to how food might change color in the freezer over time, canned goods can also exhibit subtle alterations.

It's important to note that while these factors may play a role, their impact can vary based on the specific circumstances of each canning process. Adhering to proper canning techniques, using fresh and high-quality ingredients, and following recommended guidelines remain key practices to ensure the best results.

Of course, the big question now is how to prevent this and how to deal with discoloration.

1. Follow the recommended headspace guidelines

Adequate headspace prevents food from touching the lid and causing discoloration. Refer to your canning recipe for specific headspace recommendations and adhere to them diligently.

2. Use anti-oxidation agents

Incorporate anti-oxidation agents like ascorbic acid or citric acid to counteract oxidation, preserving the natural color of fruits. When canning fruits prone to discoloration, follow your recipe's guidance on anti-oxidation agents.

3. Discard the discolored portion

If you find a darkened layer, discard that portion of the food. Removing the discolored part ensures that only visually appealing and safe contents are consumed.

4. Use the remaining contents

Despite discoloration, the remaining portion of the food is likely safe for consumption. Minimize waste by utilizing the uncontaminated part of the canned goods.

Understanding the dynamics of food darkening and implementing preventive measures ensures that your home-canned goods not only taste great but also retain their visual appeal.

CLOUDY LIQUID IN THE JARS

You reach for your favorite jar of canned goods, and something does not look right. There's a cloudy liquid in there, and you know that's not how it's supposed to look. This can be confounding, but fear not! Let's delve into the reasons behind cloudiness and discover how to keep your jars crystal clear.

The cloudy liquid in canned goods refers to a hazy or murky appearance of the liquid inside the jar. Instead of being transparent or clear, the liquid may have a somewhat opaque or foggy quality. This cloudiness can affect the overall visual appeal of the contents.

The cloudiness is often caused by various factors during the canning process. Let's explore these factors.

1. Leaching of starch and pectin

Certain fruits and vegetables, rich in starch and pectin, can release these compounds into the canning liquid during processing. These substances are tiny particles dispersing into the liquid, creating a cloudiness effect.

2. Overcooking or overheating

Excessive heat during the canning process can break down food components, leading to cloudiness. It's much like overcooking a sauce, altering its texture and clarity.

3. Types of foods prone to cloudiness

Certain foods, like high-pectin fruits, may release more pectin during processing. These foods have certain compounds that dissolve into the liquid when heated, potentially causing cloudiness.

4. Effect of hard water

Hard water with high mineral content can react with food components, leading to cloudiness.

5. Temperature fluctuations during cooling

Rapid temperature changes during cooling can influence liquid appearance.

6. Long-term storage impact

Over time, especially for high-starch foods, cloudiness may become more pronounced, though it's not a safety concern.

While cloudy liquid doesn't compromise the safety of the canned goods, it might impact the visual appeal, especially if clarity is a priority. The cloudiness can vary in intensity, and its presence doesn't necessarily indicate spoilage or safety concerns. It's more of an aesthetic consideration, and some individuals prefer their canned goods to have a clear and visually appealing liquid.

The good news is that there are preventive measures you can use to avoid your jars of food goods becoming cloudy.

1. Properly prepare food and liquid

Follow the canning recipe meticulously, ensuring both the food and canning liquid are prepared as instructed. Let the recipe be your road map, guiding you to the right balance for clear results.

2. Avoid excessive boiling or overheating

Maintain control over the heat during canning. Excessive boiling can contribute to cloudiness. Use a gentle simmer rather than a rolling boil to preserve liquid clarity.

Tip: While cloudy liquid is safe, for visual appeal, use a fine mesh strainer when serving. Similar to straining pulp from juice for a clearer appearance, this step elevates aesthetic quality.

3. Use of clarifying agents

Some recipes recommend clarifying agents like fining agents or enzymes to improve liquid clarity. These agents are tools for settling or eliminating particles and enhancing liquid clarity.

4. Handle gently during processing

Minimize agitation during canning. Gentle handling, especially when moving jars, reduces the likelihood of disturbance. Envision jars as delicate vessels; handle them with care to maintain liquid clarity.

Understanding the nuanced factors contributing to cloudy liquid empowers you to make informed decisions during canning. Exploring options like clarifying agents and emphasizing gentle handling enhances the visual appeal of your canned goods. So, fear not the cloudiness—embrace the clarity!

FLOATING FRUIT

Finding your fruit floating at the top when you open a jar? Let's talk about the causes and practical solutions for this phenomenon.

First, let's find out why this may happen.

1. Excessive trapped air

When fruit is canned, excessive air can get trapped inside the fruit's cells, causing it to float when the jar is opened. This is a natural result of the canning process.

2. Improper packing

If jars are not packed properly, leaving too much space or not eliminating air gaps, it can contribute to fruit floating. Adequate packing is crucial to prevent this issue.

The preventive measures you can take are as follows:

1. Proper jar packing

To minimize the presence of trapped air, it's essential to pack the jars with fruit effectively. This means filling the jars appropriately and ensuring there are minimal air gaps.

2. Choose ripe fruit

Using ripe, but not overripe, fruit can help mitigate the chances of floating. Overripe fruit is more prone to having air pockets.

3. Fruit preparation

Properly preparing the fruit before canning, such as removing excess air from individual pieces and using an appropriate syrup or liquid, can also impact whether the fruit will float.

4. Headspace management

Maintaining the recommended headspace in the jar during the canning process is crucial. It ensures that the right amount of liquid surrounds the fruit, minimizing the chance of floating.

5. Quality of liquid

The type of liquid or syrup used in the canning process can influence whether fruit floats. Following recommended recipes and guidelines for preparing canning liquids is essential.

If you find that the fruit has floated to the top when you open a jar, a simple solution is to gently shake the jar before using the contents. This helps redistribute the fruit within the liquid, providing a more even distribution.

Floating fruit doesn't necessarily indicate spoilage or safety concerns; it's primarily an aesthetic matter. By understanding the causes and implementing preventive measures during the canning process, you can enhance the overall quality and presentation of your preserved fruits.

SPOILED JARS OF FOOD

Discovering spoiled jars is disheartening, but understanding why it happens and how to prevent it is crucial.

Spoiled jars often result from the growth of microorganisms within the preserved food. This microbial growth is typically a consequence of either inadequate processing during canning or issues with the sealing mechanism that allows harmful microorganisms to proliferate.

1. Follow proper canning procedures

It is crucial to strictly adhere to recommended canning procedures. This includes following specified processing times for different types of foods and ensuring that the headspace—the empty space between the food and the lid—is maintained as recommended. Proper processing is essential for eliminating any existing microorganisms that could spoil the food.

2. Use new, undamaged lids and bands

The choice of lids and bands is critical. Always use new lids and bands for each canning session. This is because the integrity of the seal largely depends on these components. Damaged or reused lids may fail to create a proper seal, allowing contaminants to enter and spoil the food.

3. Regular inspection

Periodic inspection of stored jars is essential. Look for compromised seals, leakage, or any changes in appearance. This includes checking for off-putting odors, unusual textures, or the presence of mold. Regular attention to the condition of your canned goods allows for the early identification of potential issues before they escalate. Any deviation from the expected appearance and smell should be considered a warning sign.

4. Storage conditions

Proper storage conditions play a vital role in preventing spoilage. Ensure that your canned goods are stored in a cool, dark place with consistent temperatures. Fluctuations in temperature can compromise the integrity of the seals, leading to potential spoilage.

Should you notice any signs that indicate spoilage, it is important to address it immediately. If there is any suspicion of spoilage, it is crucial to discard the contents immediately. Spoiled food can pose serious health risks, including the presence of harmful bacteria or toxins. Do not consume any contents from jars that show signs of spoilage.

After encountering spoiled jars, it is essential to review and reassess your canning methods. This involves revisiting the recommended guidelines for processing times, headspace, and the use of appropriate equipment. Ensure that every step in the canning process is meticulously followed to minimize the risk of spoilage.

Discovering spoiled jars can be disheartening, but with a comprehensive understanding of the root causes and the implementation of preventive measures, the risk of spoilage in your canned goods can be significantly reduced. Consistent adherence to proper canning procedures, the use of new components, and regular inspection of stored jars contribute to a successful and safe canning experience.

UNDERSTANDING AND PREVENTING CRYSTALLIZATION IN PRESERVES

Crystallization in preserves occurs when the sugar present in the canned goods undergoes recrystallization. This process is often triggered by factors such as overcooking or an excessive amount of sugar in the recipe.

1. Use accurate sugar measurements

Using precise measurements of sugar as specified in the recipe is crucial. Deviating from the recommended sugar content can increase the likelihood of crystallization. Follow the recipe diligently to maintain the proper sugar-to-fruit ratio.

2. Avoid prolonged cooking after sugar addition

Prolonged cooking after the addition of sugar can contribute to crystallization. Once sugar is incorporated, avoid excessive cooking times to prevent the sugar from reaching a state where recrystallization is more likely.

While crystallization doesn't compromise the safety of the preserves, it can impact the texture. If crystallization occurs, you can improve the texture by gently heating the contents. Stirring during this process helps dissolve the crystals, restoring a smoother consistency to the preserves.

1. Sugar types and quality

The type and quality of sugar used can influence crystallization. Some sugars are more prone to forming crystals than others. Using high-quality sugar, preferably one with fine crystals, can contribute to a smoother texture in preserves.

2. Temperature control

Pay attention to cooking temperatures. High temperatures can accelerate the crystallization process. Maintaining moderate heat during the cooking phase reduces the risk of sugar recrystallizing.

3. Storage conditions

Proper storage conditions are essential for preventing crystallization post-canning. Store preserves in a cool, dark place with consistent temperatures. Drastic temperature fluctuations can encourage sugar crystallization.

Understanding the causes of crystallization and implementing preventive measures are essential for maintaining the quality of your preserves. Accurate sugar measurements, avoiding prolonged cooking after sugar addition, and gentle heating if crystallization occurs contribute to a delightful texture in your canned goods.

UNDERSTANDING AND ADDRESSING OFF FLAVORS IN CANNED GOODS

The flavor of canned goods is heavily influenced by the quality of the produce used. Overripe or low-quality fruits and vegetables can introduce undesirable tastes during the canning process. Imagine the flavors of your canned goods as a symphony, with each ingredient playing a crucial role. Using subpar produce is like having an out-of-tune instrument disrupting the harmony.

The integrity of the canning process relies on the quality of the supplies, particularly lids and bands. Poor-quality materials can compromise the seal, allowing external factors to impact the flavor. Think of the canning process as a secure fortress and the lids and bands as the guards. If the guards are unreliable, the fortress becomes vulnerable to external influences.

1. Use fresh, high-quality ingredients

Start with the best ingredients possible. Choose fresh, high-quality produce at its peak ripeness to ensure the intended flavors are captured in your canned goods.

2. Invest in quality canning supplies

Canning supplies, especially lids and bands, play a crucial role in preserving flavors. Invest in reliable, high-quality supplies and conduct regular checks for signs of wear or damage. Reliable lids and bands ensure a protective seal, safeguarding the essence of your canned creations.

Tip: If you discover off flavors, consider using the preserves in recipes where the taste can be transformed or masked. Baking with fruit exhibiting off flavors provides a creative solution.

Flavors can be impacted by storage conditions, so remember to keep canned goods in a cool, dark place with stable temperatures to preserve the intended tastes.

Strictly adhere to canning recipes to maintain the proper balance of ingredients and processing methods. Any deviation can lead to flavor inconsistencies.

Tip: Periodically inspect your canning equipment, paying close attention to lids and bands. Damaged supplies can compromise the seal and contribute to off flavors.

Crafting canned goods with the desired flavors involves a symphony of factors, from selecting top-tier ingredients to maintaining the fortification of canning supplies. By following preventive measures and creatively addressing off flavors, you can elevate your canning experience and relish the true essence of your preserved delights.

HOLLOW PICKLES

Canning pickles that end up hollow? I've faced that, too. Hollow pickles can be a result of using cucumbers that are too mature. As cucumbers age, their flesh can become pithy, leading to hollow spaces inside the pickles.

If air pockets are not adequately removed when packing the jar with cucumbers, it can contribute to the development of hollow spaces in the pickles. Imagine packing cucumbers into the jar as a game of Tetris. Proper packing ensures a solid, contiguous structure while neglecting air pockets is akin to leaving gaps in the arrangement.

1. Choose young, firm cucumbers

Opt for cucumbers that are young and firm for pickling. These cucumbers have a higher water content and a more desirable texture for pickles.

2. Properly pack the cucumbers

Ensure that you pack the cucumbers into the jar tightly, eliminating any air pockets. This ensures a solid structure and minimizes the chances of hollow spaces.

3. Experiment with different cucumber varieties

Different cucumber varieties may behave differently during pickling. Experimenting with cucumber types can provide insights into which varieties yield the best pickle texture.

While hollow pickles might not deliver the ideal crunch, they are still safe to eat. Consider slicing them into relish or adding them to salads, where their texture won't be as noticeable.

Achieving the perfect crunch in pickles involves a delicate dance between cucumber selection and precise packing. By choosing young, firm cucumbers and ensuring a snug, air-pocket-free packing process, you can minimize the chances of encountering hollow pickles. Embracing the versatility of these pickles in various recipes allows you to appreciate their unique qualities, even if they deviate from the traditional crunch.

IMPROPER SEPARATION

Ingredients in canned goods can separate if the jars are not packed tightly. When ingredients are not in close contact, they may shift and create layers. Tight, organized packing ensures that everything stays in place, while loose packing may result in items shifting during transit. This can also be due to drastic changes in temperature, especially if jars are exposed to extremes, which can lead to the separation of ingredients. This can cause components with different densities to settle or rise.

1. Ensure even packing

Pack the ingredients evenly and tightly in the jar. This prevents individual components from having too much space to move and settle.

2. Avoid temperature extremes

Store your canned goods in an environment with stable temperatures. Avoid exposing jars to extreme heat or cold, as this can influence the consistency of the ingredients.

3. Gentle redistribution before use

If you notice separation in your canned goods, gently shake or stir the contents before using. This helps redistribute the ingredients and restores uniformity.

Ingredients with different densities or compositions may have varying tendencies to separate. Understanding the nature of each ingredient can guide your packing and storage strategies.

Maintaining the uniformity of canned goods involves strategic packing and thoughtful storage. By ensuring even packing, avoiding temperature extremes, and embracing gentle redistribution when needed, you can enhance the longevity and visual appeal of your preserved treats. Consider the canning process as a meticulous art, where each step contributes to the masterpiece that graces your pantry shelves.

SEDIMENTS

Sediments can form when solids within the canned goods settle at the bottom. This often happens as a result of temperature fluctuations during the canning and storage process.

Sediments may also be a consequence of using low-quality ingredients. Ingredients with uneven textures or impurities may separate from the liquid, leading to sediment formation.

1. Use high-quality ingredients

Choose fresh, high-quality ingredients for your canned goods. Ingredients with consistent textures and minimal impurities are less likely to contribute to sediment formation.

2. Avoid temperature fluctuations

Store your canned goods in a location with stable temperatures. Fluctuations in temperature can trigger the settling of solids, leading to sedimentation.

3. Gently stir or shake before use

If sediments are present, gently stir or shake the contents before using. This redistributes the solids, providing a more homogeneous consistency.

4. Understand ingredient particle size

Varied particle sizes in ingredients can contribute to sedimentation. Understanding the textures of different components can guide your preventive measures.

Sediments in canned goods can be managed through thoughtful ingredient selection and careful attention to temperature conditions. Choosing high-quality ingredients, avoiding temperature fluctuations, and incorporating gentle stirring or shaking when needed contribute to the overall quality of your preserved delights. Embrace the role of a culinary curator, ensuring that each jar tells a story of harmonious flavors and textures.

SHRIVELED FRUIT PRESERVES

Shriveling in fruit preserves can result from overcooking or subjecting the fruit to excessive processing times during canning.

1. Follow recommended processing times

Adhere to the recommended processing times specified in canning recipes. Overprocessing can lead to loss of moisture and shriveling.

2. Avoid overcooking the fruit

Be mindful of cooking times when preparing fruit for preserves. Overcooking breaks down the fruit's structure, contributing to shriveling.

3. Adjust sugar levels

Fine-tuning sugar levels in preserves can impact texture. Experiment with recipes to find the right balance that preserves fruit plumpness.

If you have shriveled fruit preserves, consider incorporating them into recipes where texture is less critical, such as baking or cooking.

Preserving the plumpness of fruit in your preserves involves a delicate balance of cooking times and processing techniques. Following recommended guidelines, being mindful of cooking durations, and embracing the creative use of shriveled fruit in specific recipes contribute to a well-rounded approach. Think of your preserving endeavors as a culinary art, where each jar tells a unique story of flavor and texture.

TOUGHNESS

Toughness in canned goods is a result of the delicate balance between proper cooking and the choice of fruit. Undercooking during the canning process or utilizing overripe fruit, which tends to be inherently tough, can lead to less-than-ideal textures.

1. Use young, ripe fruit

Opt for young, ripe fruit when preparing canned goods. Young fruit tends to be naturally tender, contributing to a more enjoyable texture in the final product.

2. Follow the recommended cooking times

Adhere diligently to the recommended cooking times provided in canning recipes. Sufficient cooking ensures that the fruit reaches the desired level of tenderness, avoiding the risk of toughness.

Should you find that your canned goods turn out tougher than anticipated, consider incorporating them into recipes where texture is less critical. The versatility of these ingredients can be harnessed to add depth and character to other dishes.

Achieving the perfect texture in canned goods requires a nuanced approach involving the careful selection of ingredients and strict adherence to recommended cooking times.

Your journey in the world of canning is an ongoing exploration of refining skills and enhancing the quality of preserved creations. As you continue on this adventure, each jar becomes a testament to your evolving expertise, making every canning session a celebration of knowledge and delicious outcomes. Cheers to the joy of canning and the delightful surprises that await!

As we conclude this chapter on troubleshooting common canning issues, remember that canning is a journey of learning and improvement. With each challenge you overcome, you become a more skilled and confident canner. So, let's keep our canning adventure going, armed with newfound knowledge and determination.

KEEPING THE PASSION FOR PRESERVATION ALIVE

Now that you have all the tools to begin mastering the art of Canning, it's time to share the joy and keep the canning flame burning for others. Your journey doesn't end here; it's the beginning of a ripple effect that spreads the love of canning far and wide.

By simply sharing your honest thoughts about this book on Amazon, you're not just leaving a review – you're guiding fellow canners to a treasure trove of knowledge and inspiring a new wave of passion for preserving.

Simply scan the QR code below to leave your review:

Thank you for your help. The art of canning thrives when we pass on our wisdom, and you're playing a crucial role in making that happen.

Your review is more than just words; it's a beacon for other Canners seeking the same enriching experience with canning & food preservation. So, please take a moment to leave your mark, and let's keep the canning tradition alive and thriving.

Together, we're preserving more than just fruits and vegetables – we're preserving a tradition, a passion, and a way of life.

Thank you for being part of this flavorful journey.

Your biggest fan,
Caleb Quinn

CONCLUSION

At the heart of the captivating world of home canning lies a profound ability—the power to savor the vibrant and distinct flavors of each season, a practice that transcends mere preservation and becomes a journey through time and tradition. Together, we've navigated the pages of this book, delving into the art of preservation—an art that is not only practical but also inherently rewarding.

The essence of our shared exploration is elegantly simple: By embracing the mastery of canning, you open the door to a treasure trove of culinary delights. It's about more than just creating preserves; it's about crafting memories and fortifying traditions that echo through generations. In each jar, you seal not only the flavors of a specific moment but also the warmth of shared meals and the joy of creating something meaningful with your own hands.

Throughout this adventure, we've encountered successes and stumbles, recognizing that every misstep is a lesson waiting to be learned. Your journey, much like that of every canning expert, is a progression marked by opportunities for discovery and growth. So, commit to persevering in this canning odyssey, where each challenge conquered adds another layer to your skill and confidence.

Here are some important things to remember about home canning:

- **Prioritize safety:** Follow proper canning procedures to ensure the safety of your preserved foods. This includes using recommended processing times, headspace, and sterilization techniques.
- **Use quality ingredients:** Start with fresh, high-quality ingredients. The flavor and quality of your preserved goods depend heavily on the initial quality of the produce.
- **Measure accurately:** Precise measurements, especially for sugar and fruit, are crucial for achieving the desired consistency and taste in your preserves.
- **Follow recipes:** Stick to trusted and tested canning recipes. These recipes are designed to provide the right balance of ingredients and ensure proper preservation.
- **Remember that headspace matters:** Maintain the recommended headspace in your jars. This helps create a vacuum seal, preventing spoilage and ensuring a longer shelf life.

- **Inspect jars and lids:** Check jars and lids for any damage before use. Damaged equipment can lead to failed seals and compromised safety.
- **Adjust for altitude:** Processing times can vary based on your altitude. Make adjustments to processing times as needed for your specific location.
- **Learn from mistakes:** Don't be discouraged by mistakes. Each misstep is an opportunity to learn and improve your canning skills.
- **Mind your storage conditions:** Store your canned goods in a cool, dark, and dry place. Proper storage is crucial for maintaining quality and safety.
- **Label:** Clearly label each jar with the contents and the date of preservation. This helps you keep track of what you have and ensures you use the oldest items first.
- **Rotate stock:** Practice a first-in, first-out approach. Use the oldest preserves first to ensure nothing goes to waste.
- **Inspect regularly:** Periodically check your canned goods for signs of spoilage, such as bulging lids, off smells, or changes in color and texture.
- **Share and enjoy:** Canning is not just about preservation; it's about sharing and enjoying. Share your canned goods with friends and family and savor the fruits of your labor.
- **Keep learning:** The world of canning is vast and ever-evolving. Stay curious, keep learning, and explore new recipes and techniques to enhance your skills.

As our collective exploration draws to a close, I extend an invitation to you to share your thoughts and experiences by leaving a review. Your insights become a beacon for others embarking on their own journey of preserving, tasting, and creating. Your review is not just a reflection; it's a piece of wisdom and encouragement for those, much like you, seeking to capture the essence of time and tradition in jars.

Thank you for being an integral part of this canning adventure. May your future endeavors in the world of preserving be filled with joy, flavor, and the satisfaction that comes from creating something truly special. Happy preserving!

REFERENCES

Acidifying canned products for safety. (n.d.). Penn State Extension. https://extension.psu.edu/acidifying-canned-products-for-safety

Acids and bases. (2021, April 7). Science Learning Hub. https://www.sciencelearn.org.nz/resources/3019-acids-and-bases-introduction

Acids and bases – introduction. (2021, April 7). Science Learning Hub. https://www.sciencelearn.org.nz/resources/3019-acids-and-bases-introduction

Acids, bases, pH, and buffers. (2018). Khan Academy. https://www.khanacademy.org/science/biology/water-acids-and-bases/acids-bases-and-ph/a/acids-bases-ph-and-bufffers

Beiler, L. (2023, May 8). *Canning for beginners: Favorite basic canning supplies.* Thrifty Frugal Mom. https://www.thriftyfrugalmom.com/canning-supplies-for-beginners

Boyles, M. (2023, November 1). *Water-bath canning: Beginner's guide.* The Old Farmer's Almanac. https://www.almanac.com/water-bath-canning-beginners-guide

Brown, J. (2020, April 28). *Frozen, fresh or canned food: What's more nutritious?* BBC Future. https://www.bbc.com/future/article/20200427-frozen-fresh-or-canned-food-whats-more-nutritious

Canned vs fresh. (2015). Seneca Foods. https://www.senecafoods.com/canned-vs-fresh

Dianne. (2019, June 2). *11 potential water bath canning problems and solutions.* Hidden Springs Homestead. https://www.hiddenspringshomestead.com/water-bath-canning-problems-and-solutions

Effects of pH and acidity in food. (2021, June 17). Terrafoodtech. https://www.terrafoodtech.com/en/effects-of-ph-in-preserves-and-ready-meals

Ellis, E. (2022, October 3). *Are canned foods nutritious for my family?* Academy of Nutrition and Dietetics. https://www.eatright.org/food/planning/smart-shopping/are-canned-foods-nutritious-for-my-family

Ensuring a good seal on canned goods. (n.d.). Penn State Extension. https://extension.psu.edu/ensuring-a-good-seal-on-canned-goods

Ensuring safe canned foods. (2015). National Center for Home Food Preservation. https://nchfp.uga.edu/how/general/ensuring_safe_canned_foods.html

Ewald, J. (2014, August 15). *Canning and nutrition.* Life & Health Network. https://lifeandhealth.org/lifestyle/canning-and-nutrition/172353.html

Food preservation - aseptic processing. (n.d.). Encyclopedia Britannica. https://www.britannica.com/topic/food-preservation/Aseptic-processing

50+ pressure canning recipes. (2021, February 15). Practical Self Reliance. https://practicalselfreliance.com/pressure-canning-recipes

Freedman, I. W. (n.d.). *How to test pH of food for canning.* Mother Earth News. https://www.motherearthnews.com/real-food/test-acidity-zbcz1509

Garden-Robinson, J. (2019, July 15). *Canning food properly is vital.* North Dakota State University Extension. https://www.ag.ndsu.edu/news/news releases/2019/july-15-2019/canning-food-properly-is-vital

Garden-Robinson, J. (2019, July 15). *Canning food properly is vital.* North Dakota State University Extension. https://www.ag.ndsu.edu/news/news releases/2019/july-15-2019/canning-food-properly-is-vital

General canning information. (2015). National Center for Home Food Preservation. https://nchfp.uga.edu/how/general/ensuring_safe_canned_foods.html

Govindji, A. (2018, October 29). *10 reasons to enjoy canned food.* Love Canned Food. https://lovecannedfood.com/10-reasons-to-enjoy-canned-food

Hamilton, A. (2023, June 15). *Jars and lids are key to successful canning.* University of New Hampshire Extension. https://extension.unh.edu/blog/2023/06/jars-lids-are-key-successful-canning

Hayes, B. (2019, June 29). *7 most common canning problems and how to fix them.* Morning Chores. https://morningchores.com/canning-problems

Heldman, D. R. (2014). Food preservation: A brief history. *Food Technology, 68*(7), 26-311

Heldman, D. R. (2014, July). *Food preservation: A brief history.* Food Technology, 68(7), 26-311

High-acid foods. (2023). University of California Cooperative Extension. https://ucanr.edu/sites/inyomonomfp/Safe_Food_Preservation/Canning/High-Acid_Foods

Ingham, B. H. (2020, July 27). *Canning update: Successful jar sealing.* Safe & Healthy Food for Your Family. https://fyi.extension.wisc.edu/safefood/2020/07/27/canning-update-successful-jar-sealing

Lára. (2021, May 11). *9 canning myths new canners need to know before canning.*

Mulberry Wind Acres. https://mulberrywindacres.com/myths-new-canners-need-to-know

Loe, T. (2014, November 28). *Get to know the truth behind common canning myths.* FineGardening. https://www.finegardening.com/project-guides/fruits-and-vegetables/shelving-common-canning-myths-2

Lynn, L. (2013, August 26). *How to store home canned food for best results.* The Self Sufficient HomeAcre. https://www.theselfsufficienthomeacre.com/2013/08/how-to-store-your-home-canned-foods.html

McDonnell, K. (2019, October 9). *Canned food: Good or bad?* Healthline. https://www.healthline.com/nutrition/canned-food-good-or-bad#nutritional-content

McGlynn, W. (2016, July). *The importance of food pH in commercial canning operations -.* Oklahoma State University. https://extension.okstate.edu/fact-sheets/the-importance-of-food-ph-in-commercial-canning-operations.html

Mills-Gray, S. (n.d.). The basics of safe canning. In *University of Missouri Extension.* https://ucanr.edu/sites/camasterfoodpreservers/files/340661.pdf

Mitchell, P. A. (2022, August 18). *12 benefits of canning your own food.* Tasting Table. https://www.tastingtable.com/970739/benefits-of-canning-your-own-food

Nielsen, C. (2016, August 24). *Canning safety critical to avoid sickness.* Richmond News. https://www.richmond-news.com/living/claire-nielsen-canning-safety-critical-to-avoid-sickness-5793421

Norris, M. K. (2016, August 12). *6 canning myths you must know.* Melissa K Norris. https://melissaknorris.com/podcast/6-canning-myths-you-must-know

PH meters and home canning. (n.d.). Healthy Canning. https://www.healthycanning.com/ph-meters-and-home-canning

Pressure canning: Beginner's guide and recipes. (2023, November 1). Old Farmer's Almanac. https://www.almanac.com/pressure-canning-guide

Riggs, K., & Nummer, B. (n.d.). *Principles of pressure canning.* Utah State University Extension. https://extension.usu.edu/preserve-the-harvest/research/principles-of-pressure-canning

Rosy Blu. (2014, July 21). *Canning equipment 101: The tools you need to start canning.* https://rosybluhome.com/canning-equipment-101-the-tools-you-need-to-start-canning

Sakawsky, A. (2020, July 16). *6 canning safety rules you must follow*. The House & Homestead. https://thehouseandhomestead.com/canning-safety-rules

Storing canned food. (2012). University of Minnesota Extension. https://exten sion.umn.edu/preserving-and-preparing/storing-canned-food

The benefits of home canning. (n.d.). Alliance, OH - Official Website. https://www.cityofalliance.com/322/The-benefits-of-home-canning

The power of acid in cooking: How to use it to transform your dishes. (2023, March 8). Season to Taste. https://www.seasontotastenc.com/chefs-blog-list/the-power-of-acid-in-cooking-how-to-use-it-to-transform-your-dishes

Victoria. (2019, May 10). *7 easy water bath canning recipes for new canners*. A Modern Homestead. https://www.amodernhomestead.com/easy-water-bath-canning-recipes

Wimbush-Bourque, A. (2010, September 10). *9 reasons to can your own food*. Simple Bites. https://simplebites.net/9-good-reasons-to-can-your-own-food

Winger, J. (2020, March 10). *The ultimate guide to canning safety*. The Prairie Homestead. https://www.theprairiehomestead.com/2020/03/canning-safety.html

Young, M. (2016, July 30). *Troubleshooting common canning problems*. Farm Fit Living. https://farmfitliving.com/troubleshooting-common-canning-problems

Printed in Great Britain
by Amazon

43669433R00109